THE
POSITIVE
PARENTING
WORKBOOK

THE
POSITIVE
PARENTING
WORKBOOK

An Interactive Guide for
Strengthening Emotional Connection

REBECCA EANES

A TarcherPerigee Book

tarcherperigee

An imprint of Penguin Random House LLC
375 Hudson Street
New York, New York 10014

Most TarcherPerigee books are available at special quantity discounts
for bulk purchase for sales promotions, premiums, fund-raising, and
educational needs. Special books or book excerpts also can be
created to fit specific needs. For details, write:
SpecialMarkets@penguinrandomhouse.com.

Library of Congress Cataloging-in-Publication Data
Names: Eanes, Rebecca, author.
Title: The positive parenting workbook : an interactive guide for
strengthening emotional connection / Rebecca Eanes.
Description: New York : TarcherPerigee, 2018. |
Includes bibliographical references.
Identifiers: LCCN 2017043000 | ISBN 9780143131557 (paperback)
Subjects: LCSH: Parenting. | Parent and child. | BISAC: FAMILY &
RELATIONSHIPS / Parenting / Motherhood. |
FAMILY & RELATIONSHIPS / Parenting / General.
Classification: LCC HQ755.8 .E1763 2018 | DDC 649/.1—dc23
LC record available at https://lccn.loc.gov/2017043000

Printed in the United States of America

BOOK DESIGN BY KATY RIEGEL

CONTENTS

Introduction   vii

CHAPTER ONE   Positive Parenting 101   1

CHAPTER TWO   Looking Within First   19

CHAPTER THREE Getting on the Same Parenting Page   38

CHAPTER FOUR   Communicating for Connection   57

CHAPTER FIVE   Building a Foundation of
               Trust with Your Child   70

CHAPTER SIX   Defining Your Family Culture   79

CHAPTER SEVEN Seeing Problem Behavior in a New Way   99

CHAPTER EIGHT Raising Emotionally Healthy Children   113

CHAPTER NINE   Trading Punishment for Solutions   126

CHAPTER TEN   Top Parenting Challenges—
               And How to Use Proactive Parenting
               to Deal with Them   140

Notes   161
Recommendations for Further Reading   163
About the Author   165

INTRODUCTION

IN 2005, I received a late Christmas gift, the best Christmas gift there could ever be. It was December 26. The gifts from the day before still needed to be sorted and put away. The lights still twinkled on the tree. My feet were bare and cold on the bathroom floor, and my hands were shaking as I held a digital pregnancy test, watching the hourglass spinning round and round. When it stopped, my life was forever changed.

I spent the next forty weeks talking, singing, and reading to the baby growing inside me. As I read the book *Guess How Much I Love You*, by Sam McBratney, I would rub my tummy in circles and pat whatever little body part poked up. I didn't exactly know who was growing in there, but—*oh!*—how I loved him so. I prepared a beautiful nursery, which he never used but which was symbolic for welcoming into our lives a new family member. His name was on the wall. He had a place here already. He belonged.

He was placed in my arms in September, the most beautiful and perfect little boy I'd ever seen. The following two years were nothing short of magical. We played peekaboo and watched *Thomas & Friends*. I clapped when he learned to roll over, to sit up, to crawl, walk, and run. I marveled at each new word he spoke. We were completely and beautifully connected, this little boy and I. In his eyes, I saw trust.

We welcomed another son twenty-six months after the first had arrived, and I was once again totally and completely in love. I thought we'd carry on our days in perfect harmony until they went off to college in the very distant future. But no. Slowly, things began to change.

My firstborn, struggling with this overwhelming change in his life, began acting in ways I'd never seen him act. Back then, I called it *defiant*. I now recognize it as *disconnected*. In order to get a handle on this defiant toddler, I began putting him in a time-out. I thought this was simply the way of things. It didn't feel *good*, but it was just how it had to be, I thought.

Eventually, the days turned from being filled with playfulness, joy, and laughter to being filled with tears and time-outs. His behavior only worsened during that time. I tried all the tricks. Counting to three. Behavior charts. Nothing made things better. In fact, every time I put him in that little green chair at the end of the hallway, separated from me as I held his baby brother in my arms, he seemed to break just a little more.

I just wanted to teach him, not break him.

One day, when I saw him sitting there, eyes downcast, chin quivering, tears rolling down his still-baby cheeks, I stopped cold. Suddenly my eyes were opened to what I was doing, to his grief, to his loss and to mine. I looked into his eyes, and I no longer saw trust there. I saw sadness. My little boy no longer trusted his mommy. Not completely. Not like he had before. Traditional discipline had driven a wedge between our hearts.

My son wasn't defiant. He'd had his world turned upside down, and he didn't know how to cope. I was the center of his world, and suddenly at least half of my attention, if not most of it, was going to a little baby he'd never asked for. He felt strong emotions, and he couldn't process them. He couldn't explain them. All he could do was *feel*, and it felt really bad. Bad feelings drive bad behavior, which I then punished him for, compounding his bad feelings. It is such a messy cycle, but it's possible to get out of it.

When I finally understood that what he needed wasn't punishment but to simply feel connected to me like he used to, I completely changed my approach. I trashed the green chair and brought him into my lap. I held him and read him books. We colored together. We hugged stuffed animals and talked about better ways to deal with frustration, anger, fear, and sadness. I told him I loved him just as much as I always had, and that my love for him would never, ever change.

The brokenness was healed.

We built block towers and forts. We painted with our feet. We had water balloon fights. We danced. We sang. The trust returned to his eyes. He and his brother became best friends. There was laughter again. There was joy. There was connection.[1]

A strong emotional connection is the heart of joyful family living. Did you know that early attachment relationships shape a child's development? Your level of emotional connection with your child is a key factor in his or her own emotional development, creativity, resilience, school success, self-esteem, and behavior.[2] In your romantic relationship, emotional connection is the glue that will hold you together through the trials of life and parenthood. Your own emotional health is vital to your well-being and your ability to show up day after day and give it your best. Each of these three vital areas has a big impact on how children are shaped, and this book addresses all of them.

In 2016, I published a book titled *Positive Parenting: An Essential Guide*. This workbook makes a terrific companion to it, and the chapter outline is roughly the same, so they go hand in hand. However, you don't have to own *Positive Parenting* to benefit from this book; *The Positive Parenting Workbook* can stand alone.

This workbook is going to lead you on a journey to a happier, better connected, more joyful life. There will be some bumps along the way, and the road might get steep at times, but I know you can do this. There are so many books out there that give you a formula for raising kids without taking into account your story, your uniqueness, and your one-of-a-kind child. I'm not trying to sell you a formula. My hope is to clear enough space in these pages for you to tap into your intuition and find your own voice; because everything in this book is pointing you toward what is already stirring in your heart— your desire to feel connected, joyful, and peaceful—I believe you'll feel the weight begin to lift by the end of chapter one.

May love reign in the walls of your home and in the hearts of all who reside within them.

Positive Parenting 101

FAMILY IS EVERYTHING. There is nothing more important, nor is there anything more powerful. It is within the family that we first discover how to love, how to speak, how to relate, how to live. It is where we learn our worth and develop the concept of self. In the security (or lack thereof) of our early family lives, the foundations of who we will become are laid. Family is the place where building blocks are put down, brick by brick, interaction by interaction, experience by experience, forming the very future of mankind. Could we form this more intentionally? Have the ties that bind become unraveled in modern times? Are we too rushed, too hectic, too stressed to be deeply connected? Moreover, are the parenting methods that have become commonplace actually destroying us? Could these methods be, at least in part, responsible for our unraveling? I think the answer is yes to all of these questions, but I also think it is within our power to change it—indeed it is the greatest and most important work that we are being called to.

"One generation of deeply loving parents would change the brain of the next generation, and with that, the world."
—Charles Raison, MD, Department of Psychiatry and Behavioral Sciences, Emory University School of Medicine

Consider the implications of *becoming* the generation of deeply loving parents, not just parents who love their children—all have loved—but the generation who shows this love, unwavering and unconditional, because it isn't enough to simply feel love for our children. It must *be felt by* them. How many children have been loved yet wounded beyond repair? Children must *feel* deeply loved and valued, and for that to become the common narrative in families across the world, we must change how we treat them. Look around you. Are you happy with the state of the world? No? Then what are we waiting for? Let us begin this important work for humanity.

THE TRAP OF CONVENTIONAL DISCIPLINE

As I describe in *Positive Parenting*, when my kids were little, I realized I'd fallen into a rut. Trying so hard to meet societal expectations of what it means to be a "good" parent, I had silenced my inner voice and gut instincts. As I was constantly trying to do the "right" things, the joy of parenting was draining away.

Often, we are misguided by well-intentioned doctors, family, friends, experts, and others who claim to know what is right when it comes to our children. Like many new parents, I was advised to feed my child on a schedule and warned not to pick him up every time he cried or I would spoil him. I was told he'd never learn to self-soothe if I went to him in the middle of the night. I was in a vulnerable position, newly responsible for a human being whom I loved more than life. I wanted to do what was right. As I tried to follow this advice, my inner voice was screaming. My gut instinct won out in the end, but this was just the beginning of my struggles with modern parenting methods.

As my boy grew, so did the expectations. Toddlers shouldn't be too rowdy. They should be considerate of others, share, and sit quietly, whether at a restaurant or on a plane. Aggressiveness is a sure sign of a mean, undisciplined child. Tantrums need to be ignored. Poor behavior must be corrected swiftly. The trouble with these common expectations is that they don't align at all with a toddler's development. Toddlers are, by their very nature, rowdy. They are driven to explore, to move, to wiggle! Sharing isn't a concept they can grasp quite yet, and they are still very much focused on the self. Tantrums are the immature brain's way of handling overwhelming emotions, and aggression is its reaction to frustration. It's all quite normal, yet as a young parent, I felt the pressure to fight against it so as to raise a "good" kid and be a "good" mom; thus, I had fallen into the trap of conventional parenting.

I've come to believe that many of us stumble into this trap—well-meaning parents second-guessing ourselves instead of trusting the inner whispers that nudge us toward emotional connection. Our inner voices run counter to the conventional wisdom that holding a child too much will spoil her, soothing a crying infant at night will prevent him from learning to self-soothe, a tantruming toddler needs to be ignored, anxious or sad children need to develop resilience by learning to "get over it," and teenagers should show respect before they deserve to receive it. Listening to these messages, it's as though our kids don't have the right to be respected and treated like whole human beings until at least age eighteen, often older. Perhaps by the end of college?

In our superinformed, always connected world, parenting advice comes at us from all directions, and while the messages swirling around us might be well intentioned, they don't always steer us in the right direction in terms of what's truly best for our children—and for us. In fact, if you pay attention to the conventional wisdom of child-rearing, you'll learn to believe that children are out to push our buttons, overthrow our authority, and take over our homes. If let out from under strict rule, they will certainly run amok. Anything less than the good ole iron fist is seen as wishy-washy permissiveness.

What are some of the other negative messages about children and parenting that you believe our culture promotes? Have these messages seeped into your perception of your own kids? If so, how?

....

....

....

....

....

MY WAY OR THE HIGHWAY

My firstborn was nearly three when I began "wielding my parenting power," and that's when our power struggles began. Back then, I wasn't concerned with the reasons for his behavior; I was only concerned with changing it so that he behaved the way I wanted him to. Naturally, because I was focused on his actions rather than being attuned to his emotions and needs of the heart, our connection began to suffer. The more I tried to control his behavior, the more disconnected he became emotionally, and this created an ugly cycle for us. Is this happening with your kids? Do you find that the more you try to punish or control their behavior, the worse their behavior becomes? Then, of course, the worse their behavior becomes, the more frantically you try to control it. That is the ugly trap of joyless parenting that I want to help you out of, because you and your children deserve a much more joyful and peaceful way of living.

Of course, I loved my little boy so very much. I played with him. We danced and made mud pies. We played trains and trucks. We rolled down grassy hills and sought out shapes in the clouds. There were many beautiful moments of joy, laughter, and connection, but every time I looked past his heart, his intention, and his experience to see only the behavior he was displaying at that given moment— every time I stuck him in that time-out chair and let him cry in the name of discipline—our relationship suffered a bit. Each was a tiny break in his trust in me, and eventually those tiny breaks added up to real damage.

Describe some of the power struggles you engage in with your child. As you write, think about how you relate to him or her during these power struggles and what your child's response is to you in return.

....

....

....

....

....

POSITIVE, NOT PERMISSIVE

Are you already familiar with this philosophy, or is it new to you? It requires quite a shift in thinking and behavior, and it took me close to a year to wrap my head around it all. I went from rigid authoritarian (*Do as I say or go to time-out!*) to nice and sweet authoritarian (*I want to still control your behavior, but I'll be super nice about it!*) to permissive parent (afraid to set and enforce limits out of fear of losing connection) to finally becoming a positive parent (a gentle and steadfast guide). It was a long journey for me that required lots of studying and loads of trial and error, and the reason I became an author was to write books that simplify positive parenting. Certainly, as my children grow and change, I have to keep growing and changing as well. I don't have this parenting thing all figured out, but I have come to one truth that I believe in: Connection is the key to parenting with joy.

Many people question if this is permissive parenting, and while it is definitely not, I can see how it could become permissive without the proper information, and in the beginning I fell into this pitfall myself. After finally realizing how crucial our attachment was, I didn't want to do anything that could harm it! I felt like it was this fragile bond (probably because I'd already seen it damaged) and didn't want to do anything that might break it for good. This meant I was very soft on my limits, setting them but not really enforcing them because, frankly, I wasn't sure how to do so without damaging the relationship again. The only way I knew to enforce my limits was time-out, and that had been a disaster. I was left feeling as though I was out of options.

The way to avoid permissiveness is to understand that something *does* have to take the place of the punishment you were using before.

Positive discipline begins with gentleness and ends with instruction. What does that mean? I no longer scolded my son and sent him to time-out. Instead, I used time-in or a calm-down place where we went together. I remained tender and affectionate, allowing his attitude and heart to soften so that I could teach him. This is countercultural because we are told we must harden, disengage, or withdraw in order to "teach them a lesson." We are told that gentleness in the face of misbehavior will reinforce misbehavior, but this isn't true. Tenderness connects us heart-to-heart so that our kids care about what we have to say. Once I felt that my son was calm and connected, I did the teaching necessary to help him become more self-controlled in that area.

Yes, this took up a lot more time than sitting him in time-out for three minutes, but the improvement in his behavior—and in our relationship—was worth the extra effort.

THE FIVE PRINCIPLES OF POSITIVE PARENTING

What is positive parenting? What are its guiding principles? This is a philosophy rooted in connection. Much more than a simple method of discipline or a ten-step program to raising great kids, positive parenting offers a new way to see and relate to children, which allows us to both maintain our strong bond with them throughout all the ages and stages of childhood and to guide them to their fullest potential *in the context of* our attachment, which is the way children were always meant to be guided. Positive parenting is built on the foundation of the following five principles.

1. **Attachment.** Children are hardwired to connect on a biochemical level. If that connection isn't there, the brain may not develop

as it should. Failure to develop a secure attachment may result in behavioral problems and relationship troubles later in life.

These signs signal whether your child is securely attached:

- She is somewhat upset by your departure but trusts that you will return.
- She expresses joy when you return.
- He's generally happy to be around you.
- He looks for you when startled or upset.
- She uses you as a "secure base," keeping track of you during exploration.

Attachment is formed by being lovingly responsive to your child's needs, no matter what age he or she is. The term *attachment parenting* may call to mind images of an infant nestled in a cozy cloth wrap, nuzzled against his mother's breast, but attachment lasts far beyond infancy. In fact, we never outgrow our need for connection and security, and while it may seem instinctual to respond to the cries of an infant, doing the same for a toddler or a tween may be less so. This is probably because most of us heard phrases growing up such as "Get over it," "Suck it up," "Toughen up," "I'll give you something to cry about," and "It's not that big a deal!" There's an idea that at some point, children need to learn how to deal with those pesky emotions on their own and not bother the rest of us with them—yet how many of our problems in society are a result of stuffed emotions?

Of course, emotional needs aren't the only needs. According to Abraham Maslow's hierarchy of needs, children (all humans) need warmth, rest, food, water, shelter, safety, security, friends and close relationships, prestige and feelings of accomplishment, and finally, self-actualization. They won't reach self-actualization if they get stuck trying to fulfill the need for security or close relationships. Only when they feel that they can rest secure in our love can they grow according to plan. Loving responsiveness is the cornerstone of a secure attachment not just in infancy, but throughout all of childhood and beyond.

Think about your feelings toward loving responsiveness, especially as it relates to toddlers and beyond. Do you fear that it will create a spoiled child? What is driving that fear?

✏️

....

....

Do you believe you were securely attached to your parent as a child? Were your needs lovingly attended to or did you feel that you couldn't fully trust your parent with the "real" you? How did this shape your feelings about attachment?

✏️

....

....

....

2. **Respect.** Children are whole human beings who deserve the same consideration we afford adults. They should be treated in a thoughtful, civil, and courteous manner. Research has shown that children who have loving, nurturing parents grow a bigger hippocampus, which promotes better memory, learning, and stress response. We respect our children's minds, bodies, dignity, personhood, and spirits. Below are some ways to demonstrate respect to your child (adapted from *Positive Parenting*).

- Practice positive communication skills and active listening.
- Respect their bodies. It's probably tempting to lick your finger and wipe a smudge off his face, but would you be grossed out if someone did that to you? I would. We often unconsciously do things like swoop toddlers up without warning, brush or fix their hair without asking, and so on. A good rule of thumb is to ask yourself if you'd like having it done to you without permission or warning. It's just about bringing some awareness to the way we treat our children's bodies.
- Allow them to make choices. Children are bossed around all day, so it's no wonder we have power struggles with them. They are fighting for a bit of autonomy. Allowing them to make decisions about little things throughout their day helps them to feel like they have some control and shows you respect them.
- Be honest. While you must use discretion and not spill every detail inappropriately, there is never a need to lie to a child. If you want open, honest communication with your kids, model it.
- Apologize when you have wronged them.
- Respect their space and privacy according to your good judgment.
- Avoid embarrassing them in front of their peers or in public.
- Speak kindly about them to others, especially in their presence. Remember, children believe the things we say about them and accept them into their self-concepts as truths.

Are there ways you currently inadvertently disrespect your child's mind, body, dignity, personhood, or spirit? List them here. How could you replace these practices with healthier ones?

....

....

....

3. **Proactive parenting.** I think of positive parenting in two ways: (1) catching a potential problem before it gets out of hand; and (2) having a plan of action for when a problem arises. Proactive parenting means you address potential problem behavior at the first sign, such as when you see a toddler beginning to get frustrated with a sibling or peer and you intercede. This also means putting time into the relationship to keep the bond strong so that we have influence when we need it, and ensuring that our children's physical and emotional needs are met. Proactive parenting also ensures that parents *respond rather than react* to their children's behaviors. This requires forethought and planned action.

Do you see a problem behavior beginning to arise in your child now? What is it and how can you address it proactively?

....

In the past, have you spotted early warning signs of a problem and let it slide? What were the results, and what could you have done differently to take action sooner?

....

Are you spending quality time with your child every day to build the relationship? Are you being encouraging, playful, and supportive? If so, how? Is there more you could do to foster this essential bond?

✐

....

Is there a repeating pattern of behavior and reaction that you'd like to break? List the problem behaviors below and draft a plan of action for a positive response to your child when they arise.

✐

....

....

....

4. **Empathetic leadership.** Empathy is the key that unlocks your child's brain when she is upset and allows your reason to get inside. Correcting behavior is an important part of parenting, yet we also understand that empathy is the pathway to your child's heart and makes her open to receive your wisdom and instruction. Being empathetic means we understand the needs of our children and relate to them in a way that helps them feel heard and understood, while maintaining the boundaries we have set.

Empathy is the ability to step out of our mom-and-dad slippers and into the small shoes of our children to see their point of view, recognize what they're feeling, and relate to it. Empathy soothes and heals; it brings us together on a deep level. You don't have to give the tantruming child the candy he's demanding, but you do have to understand how important that candy is to him *at that moment* and what it must feel like for him not to get it, because when you relate to and understand his experience, you will have a gentler approach—and encourage a better outcome.

Need to flex your empathy muscles? Try these two exercises.

● *The body switch.* Imagine—really imagine—if you were to be suddenly transported into your child's body. How would you cope? What would you be experiencing? How would you see yourself (as the child) and how would you see your parent (the actual you)? Would your normal, day-to-day routine be happy and soothing or filled with chaos and frustration? How would you feel about the discipline you received?

✏️
....

....

....

● *Listen hard.* Ask your partner how he or she is doing. Don't accept simple answers such as "Fine" or "Okay." How is your partner *really* doing? Listen without judgment. Ask your child the same question if he or she is old enough to answer. Ask your friends or partner to tell you a story from their childhood. As you listen, imagine you are there, watching the scenario play out. What are you feeling?

✏️
....

....

....

5. **Positive discipline.** Moving away from isolation and punishment and toward active teaching and problem-solving methods that leave the child's dignity and positive sense of self intact is a crucial component of positive parenting. My three steps to positive discipline are:

1) **Assess the need.** Understand that all behavior is an indication of the internal state of the child. Therefore, misbehavior is a cue that there is something not working well in the child's world. There is often an underlying need going unmet and manifesting as undesirable behavior. When we assess what that need is and address it, usually the misbehavior will vanish. Of course, assessing the need is sometimes tricky with nonverbal children, but the simple act of understanding misbehavior as a call for help rather than a calculated act of defiance can help you be more compassionate in your response. Sometimes misbehavior is signaling a need for a new boundary. Perhaps your young one has discovered that jumping on the couch is really fun—but jumping on your couch isn't acceptable. There needs to be a boundary of no jumping on the couch with an outlet that allows her to meet her need for playing and jumping in an acceptable way. At other times, the need could be for new skills. A child who is hitting needs the skills necessary to manage feelings of frustration and anger, and those have to be taught and practiced. Think first about what might be motivating the behavior.

2) **Calm yourself and your child.** Undisciplined parents cannot effectively discipline children. The key is to move from emotionally reactive to cognitively responsive before you deal with the problem at hand. When you are calm, you can help your child become calm. Only then can you both think of a

rational, helpful solution. Time-in is helpful to calm your child's brain because of the close contact with you and the soothing exercises such as reading and drawing. It is simply bringing your upset or misbehaving child close to you and teaching the skills of self-regulation (how to calm down and think). Your time-in area may have comfy pillows, picture books, drawing pads, or stress balls. Anything that focuses your child's attention is helpful. No, this isn't a reward for bad behavior; it's a necessary life skill. Once you and your child are calm, move on to step three. Some children may resist time-in or prefer to be left alone. If this works to calm them, it's fine. We don't want to force separation, but giving a child the space he's asking for is respecting his needs.

3) **Teach and problem-solve.** For children younger than four, problem solving is too much to expect; the part of the brain responsible for this is still too underdeveloped. For them, holding the limit by removing them from the situation or removing the object causing the problem is enough. Teaching them what they can do instead is helpful. "I won't let you throw the ball in the house, but you may throw it in the yard." "I won't let you hit. You may stomp and wiggle the angries out." When your child is roughly between four and six, you can begin teaching how to problem-solve. You can ask the following questions to get the ball rolling: "What caused this to happen?" "How did this make you feel?" "How did this affect the other person involved?" "What can you do the next time this happens?" "How are you going to fix this?"

What discipline methods do you currently use? How are they working?

✏️

....

....

....

Do you feel a sense of emotional disconnection after you've disciplined your child?

✏️

....

WHAT'S THE BRAIN GOT TO DO WITH IT?

I'm not a neuroscientist, so in layperson's terms here's an overview of the two "layers" of our brains as I understand it, and the role they play in the parent-child relationship (for better or worse).

Upper brain: This region is responsible for more sophisticated, complex thinking. It is where logic and reasoning take place. The upper brain is underdeveloped at birth and grows throughout infancy and childhood, ultimately maturing fully in our early twenties.

Lower brain: Comprising the limbic region (the emotional centers) and the brain stem (the only part fully developed at birth), this region is responsible for our most fundamental mental and neural operations: strong emotions, instincts, and basic functions such as breathing and digestion.

This information is key in understanding behaviors such as tantrums and aggression because we now understand that the part of the brain responsible for regulating those behaviors is still very underdeveloped. Young children literally *do not have the cognitive ability* to pause and reflect. This doesn't mean that we ignore their behavior because they can't help it; it means we become their upper brain for them, providing the pause and reflection and stopping their dangerous or destructive behavior until they are able to do so for themselves.

QUESTIONS FOR REFLECTION

1. What was your perception of positive parenting before picking up this book? How has it changed?

....

....

....

2. Do you think society views children in a negative light? What messages have you been fed about young children and what they need in terms of discipline? How has it affected your parenting style until now?

....

....

....

3. Can you think of a few times when you reacted with your lower brain in a moment of anger or another emotion, only to later revisit the situation with your upper brain to solve the problem in a more rational and productive way? Would there have been a better way to handle the situation?

✎

....

....

....

....

....

JOURNAL SPACE

Jot down any notes or thoughts you have about this chapter.

✎

....

....

....

....

....

....

CHAPTER TWO

Looking Within First

WHILE IT'S TEMPTING to point fingers at our kids, our spouse, or others for the challenges we're facing at home, it's essential to take a step back and examine ourselves—our past, our "baggage," our own thoughts and feelings—to recognize the role that we're playing and how we can change it. What happened to us and, perhaps more important, how we *perceive* what happened to us play a role in how we interact with our family members today.

I'd like you to start the work of this chapter by writing your story. Consider the following questions: How was your childhood? What are the events and relationships that shaped who you are today? What have been the turning points in your life? Which relationships mattered most in forming the way you relate to those closest to you now? What successes and failures have created your current outlook about the possibilities for your future? What beliefs do you have about children and child-rearing? What shaped those beliefs?

Take some time to truly reflect on those questions, and if you'd like, talk through them with your partner. Here, I'll provide some space for you to write out your life story. If your partner is participating in this journey, they might want to write up their story as well.

....

....

Now take a red pen or highlighter and mark the parts of your story that you feel need to be rewritten—the parts that you feel aren't serving you well in your quest to be the best partner and parent you can be. This is owning your story. Remember, *you are holding the pen now*. You get to decide if you'll be the hero from this point on.

Keeping in mind the story you have just written, answer the following questions.

Where do you lay blame?

✐
....

....

What are the patterns you repeat over and over again?

✐
....

....

Why are you attached to these patterns?

✐
....

....

There are two ways to interpret past experiences: empowering and disempowering. Which experiences have you interpreted as disempowering?

✏️

....

....

Ask yourself what will happen if you stay stuck where you are. Get a detailed image in your mind of how your life will be a decade from now if you continue in your same patterns. What will your relationship with your child look like? Your partner? Will you be burdened with regrets? Write a summary of your life in ten years if you change nothing.

✏️

....

....

....

....

Now imagine that you've become the person you want to be and have been living that life for a decade. What do your relationships look like? How does it feel?

✏️

....

....

Now that you have a clear vision of the future you want for yourself and your family, rewrite your story in a way that empowers you. Write yourself strong. Write yourself capable. Write yourself victorious. Change the parts you highlighted before. Become a hero!

You will bring your new story to life by changing your thought patterns. There is a great quote by Buddha that perfectly illustrates the power of doing so: "We are what we think. All that we are arises with our thoughts. With our thoughts, we make the world." As you embrace your new story, holding to your vision of the future in which you are your best self, your thoughts must come into line with this vision. As your thoughts change, so will your actions, and little by little, the story you have just written will become your reality.

CHANGING YOUR THOUGHT PATTERNS

Do negative thoughts plague your days? *I'm so exhausted. I can't do this. Why do I never get a break? Why is she pushing my buttons today? Why can't my partner be more like that person?* Everyone has negative thoughts from time to time, but if you have them on a constant loop, it's time to change that. Your thoughts affect how you treat those around you, so positive parents really need to have mostly positive thoughts! This, I admit, has been one of the most challenging endeavors I have taken on, and I still have to work on it. I was so trapped by my negative thoughts that I was fatigued, irritable, and disappointed as soon as I woke up, before anything had even happened. I already anticipated being tired and frustrated, and so I was. How can we give our children the gift of a positive mother or father if we live with persistent negative voices in our minds?

The good news is that *we have the power to change our thought patterns*. Studies have shown that we can rewire our brains, creating new neural networks that override preexisting ones. The way to build new neural networks is to go off the beaten path—to choose a new, positive thought every time a negative one arises.

But there's another side to this growth as well. As we learn to become more positive thinkers, our children learn by our example. *If we want to raise positive thinkers, we must become positive thinkers.* Not only that, but the improved attitude and smiling face that will naturally emerge from being more positive will impact your home atmosphere, and your children will have the gift of a happy parent— and what a gift that is! As American author Robert Brault observes in his book *Reflections*, "In our happiest of childhood memories, our parents were happy, too."

Think back to your childhood. Do you believe your parents were positive thinkers or negative thinkers? What clues did they give to lead you to this determination?

✎

....

Write down a few of your happiest childhood memories. Did your parent(s) seem happy in them, too?

✎

....

So how do we change our thought patterns? Here are three exercises, with space to work through your own experiences.

Exercise 1: Identify your most frequent thought patterns. Spend some time today just noticing your thoughts. When you're standing at the sink washing up after dinner, waiting in line, or sitting in traffic, notice the thoughts that are swirling in your mind. Jot them down.

✎

....

....

....

Exercise 2: For each negative thought in the preceding exercise, write a more productive thought. For example, if the recurring thought is *This kid is always pitching a fit*, a more productive thought might be *My child is having a hard time with being patient and needs my help.*

✏️

....

....

....

....

....

....

....

Exercise 3: Work on stopping your persistent negative thought every single time you have it and thinking the more productive thought instead. Because it takes twenty-one days to develop a habit, I'm giving you a twenty-one-day progress table. Try to consistently challenge those negative thoughts for twenty-one consecutive days and note how your joy grows. Mark your progress in the following table.

Day 1	Day 8	Day 15
Day 2	Day 9	Day 16
Day 3	Day 10	Day 17
Day 4	Day 11	Day 18
Day 5	Day 12	Day 19
Day 6	Day 13	Day 20
Day 7	Day 14	Day 21

How did your life change over those twenty-one days? Are you happier? Calmer? Have your relationships improved?

✎

....

....

....

....

....

DISCIPLINE YOURSELF FIRST

I'm going to dare to say something really bold. We often ignite the fires we spend a lot of time running around to put out. In other words, we cause our kids to misbehave. Not always—they are growing and learning; they have their own minds and spirits. But they also are mirrors, reflecting back to us the ugliest parts of ourselves. The rage. The sour attitude. The sharp tongue. They listen to how we talk to our partners, their siblings, them. . . . They listen and they repeat our tone.

I saw an exchange between a mother and her almost-teenage son recently. She came at him with a very snappy tone and said, "Liam! You need to take this stuff to the car *now!*" He said, "God, *fine!*" and grabbed the box and stormed off toward the car. She turned to us fellow parents and said, "I don't know *where* he gets that attitude!"

I had an idea where he got that attitude, but I didn't dare say it. She was *in a mood*. She couldn't see that he was simply mirroring her. I can't judge her, though. I've been in that exact spot. In *Positive Parenting*, I describe how my children's disrespectful attitudes and poor behaviors were a direct reflection of my own during a time when I was stressed and doing a very poor job of disciplining myself.

We also inadvertently incite poor behavior because we get busy and don't take the time to fill their emotional cups. We allow our connection to weaken.

We let them get too tired. We allow their routines to get off track. We don't feed them fast enough. It's okay—life happens, and this is just par for the course. We aren't perfect. Neither are they. But we can extend a little more grace to them knowing that they're not intentionally being mean just to make us miserable, and we can extend grace to ourselves knowing that we are responsible for so very much and we're doing the best we can. There is grace enough for all!

But in addition to extending grace, we can improve. We can learn to discipline ourselves better. We can learn our emotional triggers and make plans to avoid them or to handle them differently, practice new skills that help us channel calm in tough situations, and be more diligent in our day-to-day routines. Before we move on to identifying your triggers, I want to provide you with a bit of journaling space. I realize this section may have put you on the defensive a bit, and that's perfectly normal. Take this space to write out your feelings. How does the subject of sparking negative behavior in our kids resonate for you?

✐

....

....

....

....

IDENTIFYING TRIGGERS

Now let's identify those things that light your fuse. Think back to a time when you felt a strong negative emotion toward your child or partner. Notice when your mood shifted. The following is an example of how one might break down a scenario of getting angry when children fight to discover the real trigger, which in this case is disrespect.

When my children fight, I hear disrespect. Disrespect makes me feel uncomfortable. I get this nervous feeling in the pit of my stomach and I begin to feel agitated. Why does disrespect cause me to have these feelings? What was I taught about disrespect as a child? What happened to me when my parents perceived I was being disrespectful? When my parents thought I was disrespectful, I was physically punished. So I perceive that my children are disrespectful when they fight, and disrespect is something that must be punished. Now I see why my alarm is getting tripped, and perhaps the feelings of fear I experienced as a child are being brought to the surface. My brain is signaling that I must take action to make it stop because these feelings are terribly uncomfortable for me. Once my alarm is tripped, I'm flooded with hormones that increase my agitation and make me feel strong and aggressive, and I feel the need to release this horrible tension in my body, so I yell.

Now it's your turn. See how far you can break down the scenario you have in your mind of a time you became angry with a loved one.

✐

....

....

....

....

....

....

....

....

Jot down below the attitudes and actions that tend to make you react out of anger or frustration.

✐

....

....

....

Now it's time to learn to *expand the space between that trigger and your reaction*. This takes real, conscious effort and emotional control, but it can be done. Just think of the self-discipline that you're modeling for your child. Isn't this how you want her or him to react in times of frustration, anger, or other forms of upset—when interacting with a sibling, a friend, or anyone else (including you)?

Here are my suggestions for expanding the space. When you feel the hot anger bubbling up inside you, try the following techniques. Experiment with them all until you find what works. Below is a table to record your progress. Add your own ideas to the empty boxes at the bottom.

Calm-Down Technique	Doesn't Work	Somewhat Helpful	Works Well	Notes
Take slow, deep breaths.				
Be active. Do jumping jacks or push-ups.				
Repeat a mantra (for example, "I choose love").				
Jot down something you are grateful for in your journal.				
Count to ten (or fifty!).				
Look at a baby picture of your child.				
Call a trusted friend.				
Step outside for fresh air.				
Use guided imagery (imagine a peaceful place).				
Read a few pages of a good book.				
Silence negative thoughts.				
Ask for a hug.				

Calm-Down Technique	Doesn't Work	Somewhat Helpful	Works Well	Notes
Reframe the situation.				
Pretend you are being recorded.				
Sniff a calming aroma, such as lavender oil.				
Focus on your five senses. What do you see, hear, feel, smell, taste?				
Press the pressure point between your eyebrows.				
Close your eyes and be still.				
Give yourself a hand massage.				

PUTTING YOURSELF BACK ON THE LIST

Prioritizing your physical, mental, emotional, and spiritual health isn't a luxury, moms and dads. It's necessary for good health. It's much easier to be self-disciplined if you're feeling well. Parents of little ones, I know it's hard to make the time. I really do. But it's a matter of being intentional, even if that means you have to walk on the treadmill with baby in a carrier and toddler watching Mickey on the portable DVD player beside you. You can make it happen if you prioritize it. I remember the days of sleep-deprived stupor, and I know you're tired! Listen to me, though: *You are worth it.* **You deserve to give yourself some of that tender love you give those kids, so do it.** Give yourself two weeks. Commit for fourteen days to put yourself back at the top of your priority list. Deep down, you know that you could read a juicy novel or jog in place for the amount of time you spend scrolling through social media. I'm preaching the truth. Fourteen days. Check it off daily, and when it's over, tell me how glad you are that I pushed you.

HOW DO YOU TAKE CARE OF EACH AREA?

Physical: Eat healthy and exercise. It's simple. Not easy, but simple. Do it for you.

Mental: Look for miracle moments (tiny arms around your neck, a stack of folded laundry, dirty dishes in the sink because you've eaten). There are miracles all around us. Also, take mental breaks. Get lost in a book for ten minutes. Depart from the screens and busyness and put your toes in the grass, look at the clouds, notice the smell of what's baking in the oven. Be present. Be still. Be mindful. Meditate. Finally, if you're suffering from depression, anxiety, panic attacks, and so on, please don't let it go. Seek the help of a mental health professional.

Emotional: Reach out to your spouse, your close friends, and your extended family. Don't let the busyness stop you from real human connection. Don't confuse a "like" on social media with real communication. Call people. Visit them, even. Exchange stories. Belly laugh in person with someone. Manage your stress levels. Kick out stressors you don't need in your life! Do something kind for someone else.

Spiritual: Whatever it is that you believe in, give it your daily regard. Acknowledge the essence of you inside your body—your soul. Read a spiritual book. Pray. Listen.

P = Physical; **M** = Mental; **E** = Emotional; **S** = Spiritual

For the next fourteen days, simply put a check in the box when you've given each area some attention that day.

	1	2	3	4	5	6	7	8	9	10	11	12	13	14
P														
M														
E														
S														

QUESTIONS FOR REFLECTION

1. As a child, did you feel that what you had to say was important? Did you believe that your feelings and ideas mattered?

✏️

....

....

2. What were your parents' reactions when you showed intense emotions, such as fear, frustration, or anger? Were you comforted, ignored, or punished?

✏️

....

....

....

3. Think back and remember your parents' relationship with each other when you were a child. What did you learn about marriage and relationships from them?

✏️

....

....

....

4. What negative thoughts play on repeat in your mind? How do they make you feel? Are they true?

✏️

....

....

....

....

5. What corrective thoughts can take the place of your recurring negative thoughts?

✏️

....

....

....

6. What are the behaviors you display that you don't want your child to pick up?

✏️
....

....

....

7. Which of your child's challenging behaviors have been learned from your own behavior? Do you ever punish your child for behaving like you? Is that fair?

✏️
....

....

....

8. How will you harness that space between emotion and response? List at least two steps you will take.

✏️
....

....

JOURNAL SPACE

This was a big chapter! How are you feeling? Write it out.

CHAPTER THREE

Getting on the Same Parenting Page

PARENTING ON THE SAME PAGE is important regardless of your relationship status. Because each parent may have different values and ideas when it comes to child-rearing, arguments over who is right can complicate things. This is why laying ground rules and coming to an agreement on the main ideas will save you from future disagreements and tension. Parenting on the same page isn't only good for your relationship, but it's good for your kids as well. When you present a united front, you are providing a sense of safety and security.

In this chapter, you will reconcile your differences and unite toward one goal: building a connected family your children can thrive in. In *Positive Parenting*, I share an exercise that I think will be instrumental in helping you achieve this goal. I'm presenting it here, with space for each you and your co-parent to respond. Write your answers on the pages separately, not telling your partner what you are writing. It is important to be honest in your answers. Once you have both completed the pages, read your answers to each question aloud and discuss them together. For obvious reasons, it is best to choose a block of time when you can be free from distractions—perhaps once the children are in bed.

During this process, do your best to respect and honor your partner. Remember, you come from different family cultures, and your experiences shaped each of you differently. Try to come to this discussion with empathy, compassion, honesty, respect, and openness. Regardless of your relationship status, *you are on the same team*, and your children need you to unite in parenting so that they can expect predictable, consistent responses from their parents, without unspoken agendas or tension. It will help the family culture you are now creating together immensely.

PARENT ONE

1. I feel that you are a good parent because:

✎
....

....

2. I feel that my role as a parent is to:

✎
....

....

3. After reading this book up to this point, I feel that positive parenting is:

✎
....

....

4. When I was growing up, my parents were:

✏️
....

And I feel that as a child I was:

✏️
....

5. Discipline means:

✏️
....

....

6. It's most important to me for our child to be:

✏️
....

....

....

7. My goal in raising our child is:

✏️
....

....

....

....

8. The number one thing I need you to understand most about my feelings regarding parenting is:

....

....

....

9. My biggest fear right now as it relates to parenting is:

....

....

....

PARENT TWO

1. I feel that you are a good parent because:

....

....

2. I feel that my role as a parent is to:

....

....

3. After reading this book up to this point, I feel that positive parenting is:

✐
....

....

4. When I was growing up, my parents were:

✐
....

And I feel that as a child I was:

✐
....

5. Discipline means:

✐
....

....

6. It's most important to me for our child to be:

✐
....

....

....

7. My goal in raising our child is:

✐
....

....

....

....

8. The number one thing I need you to understand most about my feelings regarding parenting is:

✎
....

....

....

9. My biggest fear right now as it relates to parenting is:

✎
....

....

....

The following is a good exercise for co-parents who are currently involved in a romantic relationship. Wherever we focus our attention and intention is the direction in which our lives go. I realize that life as a parent is a busy one. It's hard to find the time to connect and enjoy each other like you used to, especially in those early seasons when the children are very young. Perhaps in your busyness and exhaustion, you've become distant. Maybe it's time for a spark in your relationship, a rekindling of the mutual love and respect you once shared.

Just as you did with the previous questions, please answer these statements, this time placing your attention and intention on your partner and the love that brought you to parenthood in the first place.

PARTNER ONE

1. What I love most about you is:

....

....

....

2. I feel that my role as a husband/wife/partner is:

....

....

....

3. What I need most out of this relationship is:

....

....

4. In twenty years, I hope we are:

....

....

....

....

....

5. My favorite memory of us is:

....

....

....

....

6. I really appreciate when you:

....

....

....

7. I am proud of you because:

....

....

....

PARTNER TWO

1. What I love most about you is:

....

....

....

2. I feel that my role as a husband/wife/partner is:

....

....

....

3. What I need most out of this relationship is:

....

....

4. In twenty years, I hope we are:

....

....

....

5. My favorite memory of us is:

6. I really appreciate it when you:

7. I am proud of you because:

CONNECTION EXERCISES

To further foster a healthy union, try the following exercises:

1. Choose a few of your partner's traits that you love. Focus on those traits in the days to come; be intentional about noticing them and verbally expressing your appreciation to your partner. The more you focus on his or her positive traits, the more positive feelings will flourish.
2. Set aside a time slot a few nights a week to turn off all distractions and just hold each other. Whether it's ten focused minutes on the couch for my cosleepers out there or a two-hour lockdown in the boudoir (you lucky duck), it's sure to enhance your connection.
3. Practice active listening with your partner. Allow him to vent to you about whatever he needs to. The listener's job is to simply listen attentively, not to offer advice or judgment. Take turns.
4. Eye-gazing is a great connection exercise. Sit comfortably facing each other. Touch each other lightly as you feel comfortable. Clear your minds and gaze into each other's eyes. Maintain eye contact for three to five minutes.

THE CONNECTED COUPLE

In *Positive Parenting*, I share fifteen tips that I've learned over the past twenty years for keeping a relationship healthy and vibrant. Let's look at each of these tips as it relates to your current situation.

1. **Fill up emotional tanks.** How attuned are you to your partner's emotions? Do you pause to pay attention? To ask questions? To offer support? How often do you offer words of encouragement

versus criticism? Are you affectionate? Do you listen to your partner's dreams and goals?

Where can you improve in this area?

✏️

....

....

2. **Focus on the positives.** Think about the conversations you often have with your partner. Are they riddled with negativity? Complaints? Or do you verbalize appreciation and love? Be intentional about looking for the positives in your partner. Write down the good points you want to focus on and remind yourself of these points daily.

✏️

....

....

3. **Argue constructively.** How do you relate to your partner when there is conflict? Do you tend to give the cold shoulder? Shut down? Spout venomous words? Do you even get physical? Connected couples must learn how to argue constructively. Jot down the areas where you need to improve the most.

✏️

....

....

4. **Treat each other with respect.** Do you feel respected by your partner? Do you feel that you show proper respect to him or her? In respectful relationships, partners not only refrain from negative actions but also engage in positive ones (being courteous, considerate, and kind). How can you improve in showing respect to your partner?

✎
....

....

5. **Be flirtatious.** When is the last time you flirted with your partner? If the playfulness and flirty behavior has waned from your relationship, now is a good time to bring it back. List three ways you'll flirt this week in order to rekindle the spark.

✎
....

6. **Give each other space.** Do you have a healthy hobby? Shared interests and hobbies are good for connection, but it's also good to have time alone to just be you. What hobbies or interests make you feel at ease and offer you a healthy respite from the daily grind?

✎
....

7. **Be intimate.** I know that when you have children hanging on you all day, you can start to feel "touched out." I've been there! But it's important to keep intimacy alive both in and out of the bedroom. I'm not just talking about sex, but emotional closeness

as well. What's standing in the way of intimacy for you? How could you get back to a more connected relationship?

....

....

8. **Have fun together.** Do you have a regular date night? Schedule it on the calendar and make time alone together a priority. And as I like to say, even microwaved chicken nuggets in the living room counts as long as you're both present. What day this week will you commit to?

....

9. **Show appreciation.** We can easily fall into the habit of assuming that our partner knows we are appreciative. Even if this is true, it's always nice to be reminded that we are appreciated. We all need to feel like we are more than paycheck earners and house-keepers and that we are making a significant and appreciated contribution to the lives of our loved ones. Let your partner know how important he or she is in your goals and pursuits in life. What does your partner do that you appreciate?

....

10. **Be affectionate.** Affection is another emotional need that can fall off the radar without mindful intention. Showing affection boosts oxytocin and reduces stress. Just as we do not withhold affection from a child whose behavior we do not like, we should not withhold affection from our partners if they are not doing our bidding. Love and affection are not a carrot to be dangled in front of those we love; they are a lifeline in a loving and connected relationship. Do you feel that you show enough affection to your partner? How can you love well in this area?

11. **Be trustworthy.** Do you feel that you can fully trust your partner? Do you think your partner feels he or she can fully trust you? If trust has been broken in the past, this may be an area that needs your attention, and you may need the help of a professional. Are you honest? Do you keep your word? Are you faithful? Do you keep confidences? Do you have a habit of bad-mouthing your partner to your friends? Reflect on these questions for a moment and write down how you can improve in this area.

12. **Curb criticism.** Criticism erodes self-esteem, trust, and connection. This is as true for your partner as it is for your children. World-renowned psychologist and relationship expert Dr. John Gottman calls criticism one of the four horsemen regarding relationship killers, likening it to the apocalyptic end foretold in the New Testament. He notes that the antidote to criticism is "blameless complaints," in which you use *I* statements to express

a need. State how you feel and what you need rather than criticizing your partner, which puts him on the defensive. For example, rather than "You never spend time with me because you're always tinkering in the garage," you might say, "I feel sad that we don't spend as much time together as we used to. I'd like to schedule one evening per week to spend with you." Do you have a critical tongue? How will you work to tame it?

....

13. **Share leadership.** There's nothing wrong with dividing and delegating tasks in order to get everything done, but both parents should take part—and share the belief that running a home and raising children is a collaborative effort. Is this an issue in your relationship? Unspoken resentment in this area usually doesn't resolve itself. What do you wish you could say, do, or change about your family's division of labor?

....

....

14. **Be proactive when it comes to common relationship problems.** Differences in child-rearing, money worries, poor communication, and problems with shared leadership all erode relationships. Discuss these issues with each other before they catch you off guard. Which of these negatively impacts your relationship the most?

....

15. Communicate effectively. We are diving into this topic in the next chapter, but for now, think about how you communicate with each other. Are there improvements that could be made? Do you feel heard by your partner?

✏️
....

....

QUESTIONS FOR REFLECTION

1. Is there a harmful or negative pattern in your relationship that needs to be addressed?

✏️
....

....

2. Is your attention focused on the positive or negative traits of the people in your life?

✏️
....

3. Will you commit to looking for and pointing out the goodness of those you love?

✏️
....

4. Will you commit to reconciling your differences for the sake of building a connected family?

✎
....

Share the answers to the following questions with your partner.

5. What makes you feel loved?

✎
....

....

6. What makes you feel appreciated?

✎
....

....

7. Is there anything lacking in the relationship that you would like to resolve?

✎
....

....

....

JOURNAL SPACE

Write down any thoughts that stand out about this chapter.

....

....

....

....

....

....

....

....

....

....

....

....

....

CHAPTER FOUR

Communicating for Connection

THERE'S A REASON so many people say, "Sometimes I open my mouth and my mother comes out." How your parents communicated with you and with each other set the example for what communication is "supposed" to be. Do you see similarities in the way you communicate with your partner and children now? It can be challenging to learn positive communication skills if you grew up in a home where negative communication was the norm, but as with every subject explored in this book, change is possible if you're willing to do the work. The payoff will certainly be worth it—for you, your relationship, and your whole family.

Many of us have learned the unfortunate lesson that love is conditional. Through both verbal and nonverbal communication, we were instilled with an attitude of "I'll scratch your back if you scratch mine" when it comes to relationships. If we don't receive the behavior we want and need from the people closest to us, we tend to shut down and deny them loving treatment in return. This may be understandable, but it doesn't address the problem; instead, we react in kind, and a bond of trust gets worn down over time. But the truth is we always have a choice. We *can* take a higher road. We can choose to be loving even if we aren't feeling loved.

Let's talk about what it means to choose to be loving even if we aren't feeling loved. Naturally, I'm *not* talking about accepting any sort of physical or verbal abuse. I believe that all human beings are deserving of respect, and I would never suggest that you show unconditional love in the face of abuse. I'm talking about the ordinary conflicts—being rubbed the wrong way by someone's words, being on the receiving end of an eye roll from your child, those sorts of things. When my nine-year-old son is feeling grouchy, I can respond with my own grouchiness, I can withdraw and give him the cold shoulder, or I can let him know that I see he's feeling grumpy and I love him even so, and ask what I can do to help him shift his mood. I can help to change the dynamic rather than be swept up in it. I can take a step back and see the bigger picture, and I can react in a mature way rather than reflect the behavior of my immature child.

When I'm overwhelmed and get snappy with my husband, he gives me space to get regulated rather than "poking the lizard." Have you heard this phrase? Drs. Tina Payne Bryson and Dan Siegel use it in their book *No-Drama Discipline*. Basically, when we are angry or overwhelmed, our "downstairs" brain is "lit up," or most active. This is our "primitive" or "lizard" brain. So when someone keeps doing something that triggers us when we are already upset, the authors call it "poking the lizard." It never leads to problem solving or good communication! I've witnessed couples who shout at each other and say terrible things—poking each other's lizards repeatedly, if you will—then avoid each other for hours or even days. If we don't consciously choose how we will communicate with the people we love most, we tend to fall back on what we learned watching our parents.

Did your parents give each other the cold shoulder or silent treatment? How did they handle conflict?

✏️

....

How did you feel as a child when your parents wouldn't speak to each other or treated each other coldly?

✏️

....

COMMUNICATING WITH OUR PARTNERS

Do any of these negative communication signs ring true for either of you? Check the ones that do.

- ❖ You invalidate emotions. "It's not that big a deal. You're overreacting!"
- ❖ You clam up when strong emotions are present. "I'm fine. I don't want to talk about it."
- ❖ You yell or say hurtful things during conflict.
- ❖ You keep your emotions and thoughts bottled up and then explode all at once.
- ❖ You overgeneralize. "You *always* leave your dirty clothes on the floor." "You *never* take me out anywhere." "You forget this *all the time*."
- ❖ You lay blame on your partner.
- ❖ You criticize or put down your partner.

Of those you checked, how many were demonstrated in your home when you were a child?

✎

....

....

POSITIVE COMMUNICATION TIPS

1. "I" before "you" will help you get through. Work on replacing "you" statements with "I" statements, as this is a way to assertively communicate your need without attacking someone. Example: Instead of "You make me furious when you're late," try "I feel worried when you are late, and I begin to feel overwhelmed."

2. A win-win is a good place to begin. Looking for win-win solutions is an effective problem-solving method. The five-step process of reaching a win-win is as follows:

   ◆ **Separate** the person from the problem. You may not like your partner's stance on discipline, but you love your partner. When conflict arises, it becomes easy to let your negative feelings regarding the *problem* spill over onto the *person*.

   ◆ **Assess** beliefs, emotions, and concerns. Seek to understand your partner's point of view.

   ◆ **Explore,** invent, and rethink options. This is a brainstorming phase.

   ◆ **Agree** on a solution you both feel good about. If you're having trouble, remember to aim for key concerns.

   ◆ **Give** the solution a fair chance. If it truly doesn't work out, repeat step 2.

3. To assume makes one fume. Assumptions about what your partner is thinking or feeling can lead to unnecessary anger or bitterness. Don't make assumptions; instead, say how you feel and check in with your partner about his or her feelings.

4. Listen, listen so there's no division. Just because you're hearing your partner speaking doesn't mean you're listening. Focus your attention on the speaker. Listen to understand, not simply to respond! Maintain eye contact and receptive body language. Put away devices and distractions and don't multitask during important conversations.

5. Halt with finding fault. Criticism is a conversation killer. Finding fault, laying blame, and pointing out all your partner's wrongdoing does nothing positive for your relationship. We all have faults, but love sees beyond these faults and notices the good within someone.

6. Drop it when it's hot. When the talk gets heated, take a break to calm yourself and wait until you are able to think clearly and speak calmly. This will save you from saying something hurtful that you will regret later.

Of these six positive communication tips, which do you currently regularly practice?

✍
....

....

Which could you improve upon?

✐

....

....

What is the biggest communication barrier you feel you have with your partner currently? Can you make time to discuss this and look for a win-win solution?

✐

....

JOURNAL SPACE

Write down any thoughts that stand out about this section.

✐

....

....

....

....

....

....

....

....

....

COMMUNICATING WITH OUR KIDS

Positive communication is one of the most practical ways to build healthy relationships. This includes not only our actual words but also our tone of voice and nonverbal communication. A harsh glare can be just as hurtful as a verbal insult. A warm smile can be just as soothing as a hug. Keep in mind what you already know to be true: The method of communication we tend to carry in our lives is learned in childhood. This means you are teaching your child how to communicate with each and every interaction. You can give your child a head start on healthy communication and healthy relationships for life by teaching positive communication skills now.

POSITIVE COMMUNICATION SKILLS TO USE AND TEACH YOUR CHILDREN

Respect. Let me ask you this: If your child spoke to you the way you speak to her or him, would that be a good thing or a bad thing? Do you often bark commands, yell, or threaten? Or do you use respectful language when you ask your child to do something? The next time you take a trip to the store, observe how parents communicate with their children. Do you hear respect? *If we want children to speak to us and others respectfully, we must first speak to them respectfully.* This is how they learn.

Being respectful doesn't give kids the message that you aren't in charge as the parent. It tells them that they are worthy of respect. That's something you want your child to feel and truly believe, isn't it?

Encouragement and praise. Heartfelt appreciation and words of encouragement help children thrive. There has been so much written lately about how praise is a bad thing that I worry that we might begin to fear we will create praise junkies if we say nice things to our children. Don't let fear keep you from speaking words of encouragement, appreciation, and acceptance! Seek to give your children specific praise, such as "You're working really hard on that!" or "You are being so helpful today, and I appreciate that!" Offer encouragement such as "I believe in you," and "Keep going, you can do it!"

Conditional communication. The silent treatment is not an effective way to get your child to behave. In fact, this is not a mature way to communicate. Please don't refuse to speak to your children or be cold toward them until they come into line. Eventually, a child might stop caring whether you communicate with her or not. Instead, let your child know that you're always there, during good moods and bad. Keep the lines of connection open. They're vital, now and in the future.

Body language. Today, be aware of your body language. Do you smile often or frown? Do you make eye contact or do you keep doing what you're doing when your child speaks to you? Are you on your phone while he's telling you about his day? How do you feel when he does that to you?

Written word. Handwritten cards, notes, and journals are a lovely way to communicate your love and affection. Some children may feel more comfortable opening up to you in a journal, so offer this as an option, particularly if you have an introverted or sensitive child. This can be a special bonding experience, and a fun one, too.

QUESTIONS FOR REFLECTION

1. What communication patterns do you think you picked up as a child?

....

....

....

....

2. What standard of communication would you like to set for your children?

....

....

3. Did your parents communicate respectfully with you? How has that affected how you communicate with your child?

....

....

4. Do you have a tendency toward conditional communication—withholding words and warmth when you are displeased? Did you experience this as a child?

✏️

....

....

5. Pay attention to your body language. What do you convey?

✏️

....

....

6. What specific improvements can you make in the way you communicate with your child?

✏️

....

....

....

TRY THE FOLLOWING EXERCISES TO BUILD COMMUNICATION SKILLS

THREE-MINUTE LISTENING CHALLENGE

You'll need four to eight index cards with a topic written on each. Divide the family into pairs, each made up of a speaker and a listener. The speaker blindly chooses a card and talks about the topic for three minutes. The listener cannot speak during this time. After three minutes, the listener must summarize what the speaker has said without agreeing, disagreeing, or debating. Then the speaker and listener switch roles.

The benefit: Part of effective communication is learning to listen to understand, not just to respond. This exercise strengthens listening skills because the listener must accurately summarize what the speaker said, so he or she must truly pay attention with empathy and intention.

OBSTACLE COURSE

Create an obstacle course with scattered furniture (chairs, cushions, etc.) and divide the family into pairs, with one wearing a blindfold. The sighted partner must verbally guide the blindfolded person safely through the obstacle course to the other side of the room. The blindfolded person must use only his or her listening skills to avoid running into objects.

The benefit: This activity builds trust and listening skills.

SILENT ACTING

Two people will be having a conversation in this game, but only one is allowed to speak. Person A will speak her part while person B must communicate his lines in a nonverbal way. Give each person a copy of this script:

A: Have you seen my notebook? I don't know where I left it.
B: Which notebook?
A: The blue one. I let you borrow it yesterday.
B: Is this it?

A: No. That one's red. It's the one you borrowed.

B: I did not!

A: Maybe it's under the couch. Will you look?

B: Sure. Give me a minute.

A: How long is this going to take?

B: Geez! You're so impatient. I hate when you're bossy.

A: Forget it. I'll find it myself.

B: Wait! Here it is! I found it!

Benefit: This exercise shows how we can communicate a lot without saying a word!

Now give person B a secret emotion, such as nervousness, boredom, or excitement, to act out while communicating his lines. Have person A guess what emotion is affecting person B.

Bonus benefit: This exercise builds emotional intelligence by showing how our emotions can affect our behavior, and how that gets communicated to others even when we don't speak.

NOTES OF APPRECIATION

List three things that each family member has done recently that made you feel loved. Ask them to do the same. Write each list on a separate note for each person, then exchange notes and bask in feeling loved and appreciated. To make a daily habit of noticing the good, start an appreciation board. We use a dry-erase board, which makes it easy to change week to week. Encourage each family member to write one thing he or she appreciates on the board before bedtime, and watch as positive feelings flourish.

The benefit: Everyone learns that showing appreciation produces positive emotions in both the giver and the receiver.

JOURNAL SPACE

Write down any thoughts that stand out about this chapter.

CHAPTER FIVE

Building a Foundation of Trust with Your Child

W ITHOUT TRUST, we cannot be truly connected. Your child trusting you is essential for a secure attachment to form, and the benefits of a secure attachment are numerous, including better childhood and adult relationships, less anxiety, increased empathy, better emotional health, greater creativity, and a better ability to cope with the ups and downs of life. Research tells us that a secure attachment is the best possible foundation for healthy development, and trust is the cornerstone of this. Children who trust their parents and are securely attached to them behave better and are easier to guide and correct.

Trust isn't beneficial just for children, however. Trusting your child will have a big impact on your relationship as well and will affect every aspect of your journey as a parent. When you trust that your child will develop at the pace at which she is meant to develop, worries and frets won't be quite so plentiful. Trusting that your child is good and has the best of intentions will help you greatly in your endeavor to be a positive parent.

How does one build this essential foundation? You can foster trust with a child of any age, and it is never too late to begin. Don't worry if you feel that you've lost trust and connection with your child at this point. Remember, my entire journey—what led me to research, practice, and then share positive parenting—began because I was disconnected from my kids. It's fixable!

Let's look briefly at the ways you can build trust with your child in the various stages of childhood.

In infancy, trust is built by consistently meeting his basic needs for food, love, and affection. Get to know your infant's cues and respond to them promptly. Feed her at the first hunger cues, and as you feed her, talk softly and make eye contact. Smile, talk, and interact frequently with your baby. Give him lots of skin-to-skin contact and snuggles. Respond promptly to cries. This doesn't mean that trust will be broken if you don't jump out of the shower with shampoo still in your hair when you hear a whimper. It just means that over the course of infancy, your baby learns to count on you, that he can trust you to feed him when he's hungry, change him when he's wet, and comfort him when he cries.

Toddlerhood is the time when children develop a sense of self-awareness. During the toddler and preschooler years, you can build trust by allowing your child to safely explore her world. A securely attached toddler will be able to freely explore independently but will look to you as the secure base to which she can return. Trust is also built by keeping your promises, so if you say you will lie down with him at bedtime for an extra story or take her out for an ice cream cone tomorrow, keep your word. Your word is good now because you want her word to be good later. Listen to your toddler or preschooler. Take the time to give him your full attention when he talks about things that are important to him, and that may be the cat's fluffy tail or a rough interaction with a playmate. If we listen to them when they're little, they'll keep talking to us when they're big. Keeping regular schedules and routines is also a good way to build trust. Knowing what to expect, what comes next, and what is expected of them adds to feelings of security and safety.

Middle childhood is a stage of enormous change and growth. Your five- to twelve-year-old is gaining independence and understanding more about her place in the world. This is the time when peers begin to have a larger influence, making it all the more important to stay connected heart-to-heart. Connect by telling her stories from your childhood, which will not only help her know you better but also show an understanding of the things she's going through because you went through them once, too. Get involved in your child's world. As he nears the tween and teen years, it's no longer as easy as sitting him on your lap for a picture book or playing with toys in a fort made of sheets. Allowing him space to grow in his identity, showing trust, and not hovering too much is a big way to show trust to tweens. For the younger age group in this stage, playing with them is still hugely important. Try to refrain from correcting your child in front of her peers, making hyperbolic threats, or overreacting, as these things only serve to disconnect. Finally, keep confidences. Children need someone they can trust, and you want that person to be you!

Teens may look grown-up, but their brain development is still under way, continuing until their midtwenties. This season requires a delicate dance of letting go and holding on. Keep your connection with your teen strong by maintaining an open line of communication. Be respectful of her need for space and privacy and show her that you have faith in her to make good decisions and do what's right. This is a stage in which showing trust in your child really helps him trust more in you. Finally, respect his opinion and don't downplay his concerns.

How are you currently building trust with your child?

✏️

....

....

....

....

....

List some new ways to begin building trust.

✏️

....

....

....

....

CONNECTING THROUGH ACTS OF LOVE

You feel a love for your child that is deeper than you ever imagined. Of course you do! But it's not the amount of love *you feel* for your child so much as the amount your *child feels loved* that builds trust and connection. You love your child immensely, but if you're not speaking his love language, if you're not acting in ways that make your love seen, heard, and felt, that love may not be reaching his heart the way it needs to. When a child feels deeply and unconditionally loved, when love is not simply a word spoken but is something real and perceptible, then trust flourishes and connection deepens.

The following are some acts of love that may reach the heart of your loved one:

1. Make up a special secret handshake between the two of you.
2. Give an endearing nickname.
3. Hold hands when walking side by side.
4. Give back rubs or foot massages.
5. Offer hugs and cuddles after correction.
6. Leave notes in her lunch box.
7. Tell him why you like him.
8. Verbally affirm her positive actions.
9. Leave him cards or love notes.
10. Say "I love you" first and often.
11. Read together.
12. Create and keep family traditions.
13. Laugh and tell jokes.
14. Send her mail.
15. Make him a friendship bracelet.
16. Make her a special meal or treat.
17. Offer a blanket fresh from the dryer on a cold day.
18. Teach him how to knit or ride a bike.
19. Create a special nighttime ritual.
20. Take her out individually and pamper her for a day.

How does your child show love to you?

What does your child often request? This is a clue to what makes him or her feel loved.

✏️
....

Ask your child what makes him or her feel most loved. Write the answer here.

✏️
....

....

....

....

Based on your child's answer, how can you show your love in small ways each and every day? Write down some ideas.

✏️
....

....

....

....

List several new ways you can connect with each child.

✎
....

....

....

....

....

....

....

QUESTIONS FOR REFLECTION

1. Do you feel that you had a strong connection with your own parents? Did you trust them? Do you feel they trusted you?

✎
....

....

....

2. Can you perceive how the trust or mistrust, connection or disconnection, you had with your own parents may be seeping into the relationship you currently have with your own child?

✎
....

....

....

3. How do you plan to build trust and connection with your child starting now?

✐
....

....

....

....

4. Do you convey to your child that you trust him or her? Or do your words and actions convey mistrust? How can you improve in this area?

✐
....

....

....

JOURNAL SPACE

CHAPTER SIX

Defining Your Family Culture

THIS SUBJECT OF defining family culture is really important to me. I feel it is perhaps one of the most overlooked and least talked-about aspects of raising children, yet family culture plays such a huge role in shaping who they become. So often families just wing it. If there is no defined plan for creating the family you desire, the family culture just sort of *comes to be* rather aimlessly, and this haphazard, by-default culture may not support emotional connection and lasting bonds. Research tells us that happy families intentionally create positive family cultures, so let's spend some time defining what kind of family experience you want to create.

SEVEN PILLARS OF FAMILY CULTURE

1. **Values.** Family values are taught by example. What you live, your children will learn. Integrity, honesty, responsibility, respect, and fairness are just a few examples of what your children will pick up by watching you. It would therefore be

counterproductive to say that integrity is a family value if you rarely keep your word. You can preach family values to children every day, but the most important thing is that they see you live them consistently.

What values do you hold most dear? What values do you want to instill in your child?

....

....

....

....

2. **Dispositions.** According to *Oxford Dictionaries Online*, the word *disposition* means "a person's inherent quality of mind and character." What is your character? Your partner's? What about the quality of your mind? Are you positive or negative? What about your temperament? Are you angered easily or can you let things roll off? Are you a perfectionist?

Write down what you perceive your disposition to be and those of your family members.

....

....

....

....

Are there clashing personalities and dispositions within the home? If so, how can these be addressed and improved?

....

....

3. **Expectations.** Beyond expecting your child to say please and thank you and to pick up toys, perhaps the expectations that have the greatest impact are what you expect of his or her character. Do you expect your child to be able to meet challenges with perseverance, to overcome obstacles, to be a good person? In other words, do you show faith in these areas? If you expect your child to be difficult or irresponsible, you are more likely to get just that.

In the scope of expectations, what you expect of your partner also sets an example of what your children should expect of theirs one day. Moreover, it teaches about gender roles, which will impact how they treat people of the opposite sex as well as same-sex peers.

Your children even pick up on your expectations of government, society, people of different cultures and races, employers, and so on. They learn your expectations regarding lack or abundance, good luck or bad, hardship or blessings. All of these expectations play a vital role in your family culture and help to shape the people your children grow up to be.

Do you expect too much of your children, or maybe too little? Of your partner? Of yourself? How might your expectations of broader subjects such as society, government, different cultures, and gender roles affect your family culture? Are there some old expectations you've carried from your childhood that perhaps it's time to drop? Think about your expectations and write your thoughts below.

✐

....

....

....

....

4. **Habits.** The things we do day in and day out become habitual. There are some very positive habits such as dinner together, story time, and speaking daily gratitudes that impact kids. There are also negative habits like yelling, name-calling, and smoking that also affect them. Take a look at your family's habits. What positive habit can you add? What negative habit can you drop?

✐

....

....

Kids pick up our personal habits as well, both good and bad. What bad habits do you have that you do not want your children to pick up? What good habits do you have that you hope they *will* pick up?

✐

....

....

....

....

5. **Communication.** We addressed communication in chapter four, so review the responses you gave to the questions there. Are you making improvements? Give yourself credit for the progress you've made! Have you noticed how changing your communication has improved the atmosphere of your home? What steps could you take to improve things even more?

....

....

....

....

6. **Conflict resolution.** Although this is an aspect of communication, it is so important in shaping the family culture that it deserves its own discussion. It is vital to model peaceful conflict resolution and to teach these skills to your child. You can achieve this by teaching your child how to identify and manage emotions, use time-in with younger children and a peace table with older children (explained on page 96), and practice positive communication skills with your child, such as how to use "I" statements and the others discussed in the chapter on communication.

How do you currently resolve conflicts with your partner? With your child? Are you able to resolve them peacefully, or do you resort to yelling, hurtful words, ignoring, criticism, and other such negative communication? Write down how you can improve in this area.

✏️

....

....

....

....

7. **Traditions.** Family traditions provide common bonds and a sense of unity. Weekly traditions such as a family movie or pizza night or family meetings, monthly trips to a ball game, or annual trips to a museum all serve to take the blueprint you are about to create and bring it to life.

What traditions do you currently uphold? Are there any you'd like to start?

✏️

....

....

....

....

CREATING YOUR FAMILY BLUEPRINT

Your family blueprint is the plan you lay out for making your family vision a reality. Home builders do not just start throwing scraps of material together and hope the house turns out decent. They have a detailed plan and follow it meticulously. Whatever it is you want to build in your life, it helps to create a detailed blueprint—a plan for making it happen. Drawing up your blueprint, or mission statement, will help you define your family's goals and values, and indeed, your legacy. It will serve as not only a reminder to each family member but also a code of conduct that you can refer to as a teaching tool with your children. Each family member should take part in drafting the blueprint, and doing so will ensure everyone's voice is heard. Here are the three steps I recommend for defining your family's vision together.

1. Have an initial family discussion about your values, beliefs, morals, dreams, and goals. Each member must engage in the conversation. It's important that everyone is heard and respected. Write down everyone's answers in this initial meeting—all of them.
   a. List the values of each member.
   b. List the beliefs of each member.
   c. List the goals of each member.
2. Once you have a comprehensive list of everyone's values, beliefs, and goals, hold another family meeting to really nail down that which is most important and agreeable for everyone. Write out your mission statement.
3. Use the flowchart on page 87 to show how you intend to live out or act on those values, beliefs, and goals.

HERE ARE SOME CONVERSATION STARTERS TO OPEN YOUR FAMILY DISCUSSION:

1. What kind of family do we want to be?

✏️

....

....

2. What values will we uphold?

✏️

....

....

3. What kind of atmosphere do we want in our home?

✏️

....

....

4. What kind of relationship do we want to have with one another?

✏️

....

....

5. Who inspires us and why?

✏️

....

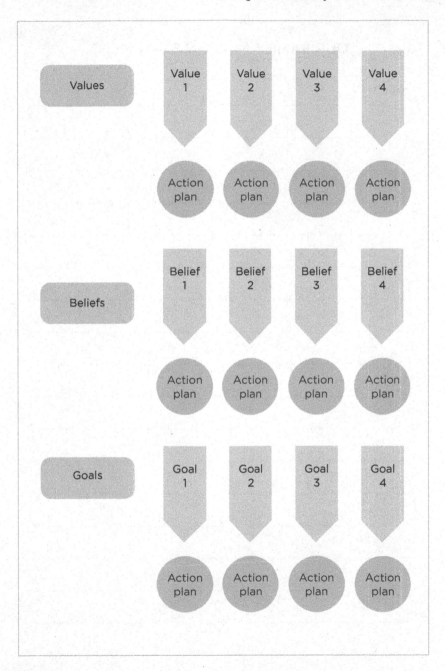

OUR FAMILY MISSION STATEMENT

CREATING POSITIVE AND COMFORTING RHYTHMS

Your family blueprint may be drafted at the table, but it is the daily routines—the ins and outs of life each day—that truly define your family culture. Regular, predictable routines provide comfort to children and may help mitigate meltdowns. When your child eats, sleeps, naps, plays, reads, and snuggles in a predictable pattern, it simply makes life easier for everyone. Of course, it's impossible to maintain a routine every single day. There are trips that must be made, visits from friends and family, and unforeseen issues that crop up on occasion. Weekday routines differ from weekend routines, especially when kids enter school. This is why I prefer the term *rhythm*. It's more of a daily flow than a rigid schedule.

Giving your child age-appropriate choices and control over her daily rhythm will help to eliminate power struggles. For toddlers, that means letting them choose their clothing during morning dressing.

For teens, it means standing back and allowing them to make appropriate choices, offering guidance only when it's truly needed.

Generally, you will want to create a morning rhythm that includes getting dressed, eating breakfast, brushing teeth, and gathering backpack and school items. An afternoon rhythm will be dependent on the child's age and the family preferences, but could include craft time, playtime, cleanup, lunch, and music. An evening rhythm might include cleaning up, a warm bath, and a story. Rhythms are as unique as individuals, and the goal is to simply find one that feels good for your family.

Do you currently have a rhythm in place? Is it working? How could you improve it?

....

....

....

....

....

....

....

....

....

LOVING RITUALS

Loving rituals become cherished memories for children. Here are some daily rituals that enhance connection:

START THE DAY WITH A MORNING KINDNESS

Mornings can be a real hassle. Trying to get everyone up and out the door on time is often a stressful time for families. Our adult minds are focused on the dozens of things we must accomplish in the next twelve hours, and our children are often tired, grumpy, or preoccupied with their own thoughts about the day ahead. Taking two or three minutes in the morning to focus on our child's face and say something positive can really have a big impact. "Good morning, my love! Seeing your sweet face makes me happy" is a thoughtful way to greet a child into his day. I think, *Triple A to start the day.* That stands for attention, affection, and affirmation. Aim to give your child your full attention for at least a couple of minutes, offer a hug or rub on the head, and say something positive about him. Making this a daily habit starts each day off on the right foot.

AFTERNOON OR AFTER-SCHOOL GATHERING

Do the children get home from school and scatter in every direction? Mine tend to do that. Even if you homeschool or your children are still very young, creating an afternoon or after-school gathering provides another connection point in your day. Some ideas for this gathering include tea time, a spread of fruits with dip or cheese and crackers, a round of Uno, or reading aloud a chapter from a great book. Again, this is undistracted time spent with your loved ones and it takes only a few minutes of the afternoon. This can easily be adjusted to an after-dinner or before-bath gathering. The time on the clock is not important. It's the time spent together that matters.

A MEAL AT THE TABLE

When my children were very little and my husband worked odd shifts, we never ate together. I would snack throughout the day, my kids would eat dinner in the playroom, and my husband just ate whenever he got home. So I certainly understand that dinner at the table every single night is not suitable for all families. Perhaps an early-morning breakfast together is more doable, or even a late-evening dessert-only meeting in the kitchen. Research from Cornell University suggests that the benefits from family meals are many, including healthier eating for kids, improved psychological well-being, greater academic achievement, and even less delinquency![3] We don't need studies to tell us that gathering together for conversation and a good meal is meaningful, though, do we? If it's not already on your priority list, now is a great time to start this connection-building habit. Once a day? Once a week? What can you and your family commit to try?

ONE-ON-ONE TIME AT BEDTIME

In my house we call this "special time," and I am surprised by how much my children crave this individual attention, because until very recently, I was with them all day, every day as a homeschooling mom! I created this habit when they started attending school to build in some special time to hear about their days, so they don't have to talk over each other or be interrupted. I initially set it at ten minutes per child, but we often talk well beyond that because children really do open up their hearts during this time. If they don't have much to talk about, which is rare, I ask them three questions: "Tell me something good that happened today." "Is there anything you're worried about or want to ask?" "Tell me something you're looking forward to this week."

List the rituals you currently have and some you'd like to begin.

✏️

....

....

....

....

....

A CULTURE OF PEACE: TAMING SIBLING RIVALRY

In *Positive Parenting*, I opened up about some of the mistakes I'd made that actually fueled sibling rivalry in my home. The first mistake I made was comparing my two boys. Although I knew in my mind that comparing them wasn't a good idea, sometimes my mouth didn't seem aware of what my brain knew. Occasionally I'd let something slip like "Your brother was potty trained by now, so why are you making this so difficult?" You can imagine how helpful that was both for potty training my younger son and for fostering positive feelings between them. Another mistake I made was labeling. Were you and your siblings labeled growing up? Was there a "smart one" or an "athletic one?" It seems I accidentally labeled one of my boys "the funny one." I didn't do this by announcing, "Wow, you're so funny and your brother isn't!" It happened rather covertly simply because I laughed at him more. This was a tricky situation because "the funny one" started doing over-the-top antics to retain his crown and got upset if I laughed at his brother's jokes. The brother would often ask, "Am I funny, too?" and sought to measure up to "the funny one." The fix for this wasn't to stop laughing at my child's hilariousness but to find something about his brother that we brought to light together and celebrated.

Are you making the same mistakes I made? Do you compare your kids? Do you label them? Even loving, well-meaning parents can inadvertently fall into these bad habits, which actually fuel rivalry.

List some ways you may be accidentally fueling sibling rivalry.

✎

....

....

....

TO HELP SIBLING BONDS IMPROVE

Over the years of parenting close-in-age boys, I have found a few things that strengthened their bond. I learned how to create more peace and discovered ways to put out the fires I had unintentionally set with comparisons and labels. It's important that when creating positive family cultures, we work hard to create a culture of peace among all family members, including siblings. While many brush it off as normal teasing and believe that sibling rivalry is just par for the course, I believe it serves our families well to be diligent in this area.

Yes, children will argue, as do all humans in close relationships, but helping them to build a positive, peaceful, healthy bond will benefit them for a lifetime.

1. **Acknowledge the bond.** Point out when they are playing nicely, getting along, and being pleasant. One tool I've used is a "fuzzy jar" for each of my children. When I heard one brother say something encouraging or kind, I put a fuzzy pom-pom in his jar. If they played nicely together, I'd give them each a pom-pom. When the jars got full, they'd get a treat. Even though I'm not generally a parent who relies on rewards, I do find them helpful boosters sometimes to nix bad habits.

2. **Create a team atmosphere.** If your kids are young, you might want to ditch individual chore charts and go for a team chart instead. They complete tasks together rather than competing for check marks and stickers.

3. **Set clear limits.** Let them know that teasing, name-calling, aggression, and put-downs will not be tolerated. Make sure the consequences for such actions are clear and that you follow through with them. When a consequence is needed, consider the following positive discipline tools.

POSITIVE DISCIPLINE TOOLS FOR SIBLING SPATS

1. **Time-in.** This is best for a young child who has aggression issues or high emotions. Bring the child into a calming space and give him tools such as books, crayons and paper, or a stress ball to squeeze so that he learns coping mechanisms for when he's emotionally overwhelmed. Once he is rational again, discuss how better to handle anger.

2. **Cool-off.** Now that my boys are older, aggression is rarely an issue, but I will send an aggressive child to his room or another area of the home to calm down. By this point, we've gone over calming techniques and problem solving enough that he doesn't need my help with it—he just needs the space to do it.

3. **Peace table.** This is where the arguing children come together with your help to learn peaceful conflict resolution. Allow each child to state her case, ensure you understand the problem, and help them come to a resolution.

4. **Repair.** I always make sure that the boys repair their relationship after an argument. Whether they choose to give a verbal apology, write a card, or make a small gift, I strongly encourage them to apologize and right their wrongs.

5. **Refer to your blueprint.** Remember how I said earlier that your blueprint would serve as a code of conduct that you could refer to? This is the time to bring it out and go over it with your child: "In the family mission statement we all signed, we agreed that kindness was our big value. Did you act in a kind way? What could you have done differently?"

QUESTIONS FOR REFLECTION

1. Are your current expectations, habits, and attitudes in line with your values?

....

....

2. What does your family do regularly that could run more easily and smoothly with the introduction of a rhythm?

✏️

....

....

3. What, if anything, is preventing you from establishing a daily rhythm?

✏️

....

....

4. List at least five rituals that you'd like to incorporate into your family culture.

✏️

....

....

5. Do you occasionally compare your children to each other? How can you intentionally keep from making comparisons that fuel rivalry?

✏️

....

....

6. It's important to look for and acknowledge positive sibling interaction. Do you do this already? Will you make it a point to do it
   daily and note any changes for at least one week?

✐
....

....

JOURNAL SPACE

✐
....

....

....

....

....

....

....

....

....

....

CHAPTER SEVEN

Seeing Problem Behavior in a New Way

I N *POSITIVE PARENTING*, I admitted a painful truth: There was a time when I was so focused on behavior management that I couldn't see the beauty of the human being in front of me. Because I was intent on correcting every misbehavior, my son's compassionate heart, the way he tenderly treated his brother and me, his sensitive soul, and all the light within him were largely missed.

Luckily, I came to my senses in a fairly short amount of time, but I'm not the first parent—or the last—to home in on discipline so intently that the *good* and the *beauty* and the *joy* go unnoticed. We are, in fact, smothered with messages about how we must get a handle on our children when they are young or there will be hell to pay for years.

Our culture is constantly feeding us negative ideas about children. When they are infants, we see them as blessings, gifts. We are quick to gush over newborn babies and how "innocent" and "sweet" they are. Oh, but wait just a few months and the message begins to change. Right about the time they learn to walk and talk, the warnings start to come. "He's walking? You're in trouble now." "Just wait, the terrible twos are coming." "Terrible twos? Ha! Threenagers are way worse." "Oh yeah, just wait until he's a teen!"

We are constantly told about how they will manipulate us, test our authority, push our buttons, and see what they can get away with. With the dire warnings come loads of advice telling us the best way to control our little tyrants—so they don't control us.

Did the "terrible twos" message cause you fear or anxiety? If your child is two or older, do you think this influenced how you saw or interacted with your child during this stage? Were you looking for "terribleness"?

✐
....
....
....

List any positive messages you've heard about child-rearing. How many can you come up with?

✐
....
....

BECOMING A LIGHT REFLECTOR

These toxic cultural messages poison our minds and negatively affect the way we see and therefore relate to our children. The clamor of the world drowns out the whispers of our hearts, and we end up viewing our children not so much as our gifts anymore but as *mischief to be managed.* In our earnest efforts to train them in appropriate behavior, we end up reducing children to little more than that, as though their behavior at any given moment is what defines them—good, bad, or something in between. As I've pointed out, our kids are more than their ability to sleep through the night. They are more than their willingness to instantly obey. They are more than a grade. They are more than a mood. They are more than a snapshot of how well they behaved that day, more than what we see on the surface. They are human beings—messy and beautiful, wild and compassionate, and worth getting to know, not just getting to *mind.* When we reduce them to the behavior they currently display, we miss out on seeing their beauty, their light, and ultimately their potential.

If we can correct, teach, and guide our children from a position of seeing the light within them rather than their momentary setbacks, how much higher will they reach? I call this being a *light reflector* because we intentionally look for the light in them and reflect it back so they can see it, too. After all, children come to see themselves the way their parents see them.

> What they see reflected in our eyes is often what they will become.

Will you be the person in your child's life who always sees her light and reflects it back to her? That starts with looking for positive motives, even when she does something "bad." Seeing your children's motives as negative ("He's trying to test me" or "She's just pushing my buttons") triggers your own negative reactions. As a result, you may become angry, embarrassed, or frustrated. In that triggered state, you may justify making her feel bad because in your mind you're doing it to make her a better person in the long run. So you scold her for her wrongdoing, highlighting her character flaws and making her feel bad about herself. Unfortunately, when she sees her "badness" in your eyes, she may come to see herself as bad—not just her *behavior*, but *herself*. If that works its way into her self-concept, she'll repeat the bad behavior because *we behave how we see ourselves*. See the person, the heart and soul, behind the screams, the eye rolls, the tantrums, the messy rooms, and the bad attitude. See their light and draw it out.

If, on the other hand, you choose to see positive intent, you see that she's a good person who needs guidance on this issue. You still correct the behavior, but you approach her with a different tone and attitude, changing your language so that you're reflecting her light. Remembering that she is a good person with positive motives who made a poor choice allows you to bring compassion to your correction, and that allows her to take it in without damaging her developing self-concept. Let's look through two different lenses at the same scenario.

Mason comes running to tell you that his sister, Mia, spilled the red juice she was drinking. Mia says she did not! Her lips are red, so you know she's been drinking red juice, and the spill is in her room where she has been playing while Mason has been with you making sandwiches. Mason discovered the spill when he went to Mia's room to call her for lunch.

Negative intent: You think, *She's a sneaky little liar!* You say, "You liar! I see the juice stains on your mouth! Mason was honest. Why wouldn't you just be honest with me? I'm very disappointed in you. It's wrong to lie."

"Liar" is not a label you want to stick. If a child thinks she's a liar, she'll be a liar. Then if she gets punished for being a liar, she'll become a sneaky liar. Self-fulfilling prophecy! You just created what you feared.

Positive intent: You think, *She doesn't want to get in trouble or disappoint me.* You say, "Hmm. I see cherry red lips. I value your honesty. Were you drinking juice and it accidentally spilled? Sometimes I spill things by accident. No big deal. We just need to clean it up. Come help me."

Doesn't the tone feel much different in each scenario? The first one probably leaves Mia feeling like a terrible person. She may feel a bit of guilt in the second one for spilling the juice, but she certainly doesn't get shamed or berated. She cleans up her mess, and you move on.

Let's turn our attention to Mason for a moment. He's just "turned in" his sister for spilling the juice. Here is an opportunity to foster rivalry and reinforce tattling, which is exactly what happens in scenario one. He gets the praise for being honest. Now he might look for more opportunities to turn in his sister. She's not only feeling bad about herself, but I'd bet she's feeling resentful toward her brother, too. In scenario two, Mason simply witnesses a problem being solved. Because he sees that problems are something to be solved, not punished, he learns there's no value in tattling. Furthermore, no sibling rivalry is fueled, because Mason is left out of the conversation you have with Mia.

How can you assign positive intent to bad behavior? The difference is in being mindful of the thoughts that arise when you see "bad" behavior. It is your thoughts about what is driving your child that will determine how you feel and, as a result, respond to the issue. Let's try a few exercises to help you switch your lens. Let's look at how the intent you perceive determines the action you take.

WHAT IS THE INTENT WHEN A CHILD HITS HIS BROTHER?

Negative intent: He is a naughty child trying to hurt his sibling.

Action: Believing he is acting maliciously will likely incite anger, or at least frustration, in you. This could cause your tone to be sharp. You might verbalize your thoughts, calling him "mean" or "naughty," and you'll likely feel he needs some sort of punishment. You may place him in time-out, where he either tantrums or keeps getting up, provoking a power struggle.

The child learns: He is bad or mean. His parent is mad at him. He may believe his brother is favored.

Positive intent: He is needing attention or direction and asking for it in an immature way, as children do. He doesn't have the words to express his needs.

Action: Because you see that his aggression is a signal for help, you aren't moved to anger. You are able to address his action calmly. You now view him as an immature child needing guidance rather than a mean child needing punishment, so guidance is what you give. You bring him onto your lap and tell him that you won't allow him to hit and that you will help him calm down. You might look through a book or practice counting to ten while taking big breaths. Then you can tell him that being upset is okay, but hitting his brother is not. You'll tell him two or three things he can do when he's upset, practice them, and then ask him how he can make it up to his brother.

The child learns: Hitting is not an acceptable release of anger. His parent is on his side. How better to handle anger. How to apologize and repair relationships. Emotional intelligence.

WHAT IS THE INTENT WHEN A CHILD IS HAVING A TANTRUM?

Negative: She is manipulating her parents to get her way.

Action: If you feel manipulated, you will likely follow the common advice to ignore her to prove that she has no power over you.

The child learns: Mistrust. Being ignored by one who loves you hurts deeply, and when you feel you can't depend on someone to pay attention to you in your time of need, mistrust forms. She also learns that she is accepted (she may see this as loved) by you only when she is "good."

Positive: She is a very young, immature person struggling with a heavy load of emotions and needs the help of an adult to wade through them.

Action: Seeing a child as needing help doesn't move you to ignore her but to actually move in closer and offer support. If a child is kicking and screaming and you can't move in physically, you remain emotionally tuned in and available. "I'm here if you need a hug." Otherwise, you embrace her while her sobs subside and her breathing slows.

Note: Some parents fear this will reward a child's tantrum, but being emotionally supportive isn't a reward; it's a lifeline. What you wouldn't do is give her the cookie or the toy that caused her to feel those big emotions in the first place. Then she may begin to have "fake" tantrums to get her way. Even fake tantrums don't have to be ignored. You can remain loving and warm while holding your initial boundary.

The child learns: She is loved unconditionally. Her parent will be there for her when she feels out of control or upset. Trust.

PRACTICE

Write some common behavior problems your child exhibits and see if you can find a positive intent.

PROBLEM: _____

_____

Negative intent:

✐
....

....

Action:

✐
....

....

Your child learns:

✐
....

Positive intent:

✐
....

....

Action:

✐
....

....

Your child learns:

✐
....

....

PROBLEM: _____

_____

Negative intent:

✐
....

....

Action:

✐
···

···

Your child learns:

✐
···

Positive intent:

✐
···

···

Action:

✐
···

···

Your child learns:

✐
···

PROBLEM: _____

_____

Negative intent:

✐
....

....

Action:

✐
....

....

Your child learns:

✐
....

Positive intent:

✐
....

....

Action:

✐
....

....

Your child learns:

✏️
....

QUESTIONS FOR REFLECTION

1. Are you currently so focused on behavior that you're missing your child's light? Have you had this problem in the past? Has your partner?

✏️
....

....

....

2. What light do you see in your child(ren)? List their good qualities here so that you can begin to focus on them more.

✏️
....

....

....

....

....

....

....

....

3. How does your perception of the intent of your child's actions affect your own emotional response?

....

....

....

....

4. How does your emotional response affect your actions?

....

....

....

....

5. How do your actions affect your child's self-concept and your connection?

....

....

JOURNAL SPACE

CHAPTER EIGHT

Raising Emotionally Healthy Children

I THINK A GOOD PLACE to start with this chapter is to define emotional health. Simply put, emotionally healthy children are in control of their thoughts, feelings, and behaviors. This is, of course, a skill that takes years to develop and master. Good emotional health means one can manage both positive and negative emotions. It doesn't mean the absence of sadness, fear, or struggle. Rather, it involves the ability to move through negative emotions and bounce back. It is akin to good emotional intelligence (EI), which has been shown to increase happiness and success throughout life. Good emotional health allows you to realize your full potential.

How can we raise our children to know and understand their emotional worlds? We can begin by helping them label their feelings from a very young age. "It looks like you're sad that you lost your teddy bear." "You seem angry that Amy has your toy." By naming these feelings, you're helping them to put words to their emotions. Punishing or shaming them for big emotions doesn't help them learn to process them. It actually only piles on more big emotions! Disapproving of or punishing anger, frustration, fear, or other difficult emotions won't stop your child from having them, but it may force him to shove them down. Instead, it's helpful to be an empathic, calm presence through the emotional storms. Research shows that simply empathizing with children—showing that you understand—increases their emotional intelligence.

Here are two games you can play with your child to boost EI.

MIRROR, MIRROR

A fun way to boost your child's emotional intelligence is to have him look in a mirror and ask him to make the faces he would make in the following situations.

1. You dropped your ice cream cone. (sad)
2. You're going on vacation. (excited)
3. Your friend can't come over. (disappointed)
4. You hear a frightening noise. (scared)
5. Someone snatched your toy away. (anger)
6. You're opening a gift. It's what you've been wanting! (surprised)
7. You can't tie your shoes. (frustrated)
8. You've been running for an hour. (tired)
9. You just ate something really gross. (disgusted)
10. You have absolutely nothing to do. (bored)

This exercise has several benefits. It increases your child's vocabulary beyond mad, sad, and happy as she explores a wide range of emotions. It helps her to recognize the emotions of others by their facial expressions. She is learning through playful interactions with you. Look up a list of emotions and make up your own scenarios to continue growing your child's vocabulary!

ACT IT OUT

Ask your child to act out situations that make him feel this way:

Happy. Worried. Sad. Excited. Scared. Frustrated. Cheerful. Angry. Proud. Embarrassed. Disappointed. Shy. Nervous. Tired. Surprised. Anxious. Calm. Stressed. Hopeful. Fascinated.

This exercise will help him link his emotions to the particular circumstances and opens up dialogue on how situations affect our emotions and how to stay in control of them.

THE ROLES OF SELF-IMAGE AND SELF-ESTEEM ON EMOTIONAL HEALTH

In an essay titled "Does Self-Esteem Function as an Emotional Immune System?"[4] Guy Winch, PhD, asserts that a variety of studies have begun to demonstrate that self-esteem can arm us with emotional resilience as well as insulate us from stress and anxiety. Brain scans have shown that rejection is more painful for people with low self-esteem than for those with high self-esteem. A child with higher self-esteem is better prepared to manage failure, rejection, and stress and has increased self-control.

It may surprise you to learn that self-esteem doesn't come from giving children trophies and stickers or by telling them they're the greatest, smartest, or most wonderful people on the planet. Instead, research shows that self-esteem grows from feeling capable and understood.

Are there some things you do for your child that she could do for herself? Can you step back and empower her to accomplish them on her own?

✏️

....

....

Seeing the result of hard work makes children feel effective. Making a positive difference in the lives of others also boosts self-esteem. Think of one thing you can encourage your child to do that will bring about this result. Volunteering? Taking music lessons?

✏️

....

Children get a self-esteem boost when they feel accepted by their parents, caregivers, and peers. Many of the things covered in this workbook will help your child feel accepted—empathizing with his emotions, communicating with respect, using positive discipline, spending one-on-one time with him, and so on. Write down a few encouraging phrases you can tell your child to convey how much you love just who he is.

✏️

....

....

Unconditional love is important to the emotional health and positive self-worth of our children. Psychologist Carl Rogers understood the need for unconditional love, or what he called *unconditional positive regard*. He believed that childhood experiences are one of the two primary sources that influence a person's self-image, the other one being evaluation by others. Self-worth, according to Rogers, is first formed from the interactions the child has with his or her mother and father. He also believed that we need to feel valued and respected, be shown affection, and feel loved, and he made the distinction between unconditional and conditional positive regard. In conditional positive regard, a child receives approval only when performing to the parents' expectations of behavior. If approval is withdrawn when a child makes a mistake, she is loved not for who she is but on the condition that she behave in a way that makes her parents happy. Of course, parents don't really stop loving their misbehaving children, but from the child's perspective, approval and love are indistinguishable. This isn't to say that a parent must show approval for the child's behavior at all times. That would be irresponsible parenting. It's to say that *we must show approval for the person even as we show disapproval for the behavior.*

Think of the discipline methods used by you or your friends. Do they convey conditional positive regard? This is actually what time-out draws its strength from—the child's fear of disapproval and separation. Time-outs work because they alarm a child into behaving so as not to lose Mommy's or Daddy's love. That's really quite sad when you think about it. Shame and humiliation are becoming trendy tactics that often earn the parent a pat on the back or five minutes of fame. Think about the children who are forced to walk in public wearing signs with negative messages, or the ones humiliated on social media by their own parents. These trends are harming the emotional health of our children.

CONSIDER SOME OF THE QUESTIONS OF A CHILD'S HEART:

* Am I accepted?
* Do you love me even when I break a rule or show defiance or have an epic tantrum? You say you do, but do I feel it?
* Are we connected?
* Do you see my light, even when I'm not shining it?
* Can I trust you with my big feelings?
* Will you be my loving guide?
* Will you always have my back?
* Can I count on you to be there even when it's inconvenient for you?
* Do you respect me even though I am little?
* Can you handle me when I am at my worst?

Unconditional positive regard asks, "Will you show me that you really love me through it all?"

Dr. Gordon Neufeld, of the Neufeld Institute, conveys this message perfectly. He says: "Unconditional parental love is the indispensable nutrient for the child's healthy emotional growth. . . . Ways have to be found to convey the unacceptability of certain behaviors without making the child herself feel unaccepted."

So here's the big question: How do we convey the unacceptability of certain behaviors without making the child herself feel unaccepted? First we have to release the fear that we are being "too easy" on children by showing our love, warmth, and affection *even when* they bring their "least likable characteristics" or behaviors. **We have to drop the fear that our love will reinforce negative behavior and accept that it gives our children emotional and psychological rest and fosters emotional health.**

Next, we change our language. We have to leave out personal

criticism and attacks. No shaming. No humiliation. State what is wrong with the *behavior*, not what is wrong with the *child*. And very important, show him how he can save face, fix his mistake, make amends, and do better. Repair afterward by connecting with him and making sure he knows that you still see his light and that you still believe in him. When he is assured that you see his worth, it helps him see it, too. For example, rather than saying, "Your room looks like a pigsty. Why are you so messy?" you can simply say, "It looks like your room needs tidying up." Instead of "Quit being stingy and share your toys," try simply stating, "It looks like your friend wants a turn."

You may need to also change your approach. Instead of withdrawing, you engage. Rather than sending your child away, you invite her closer. Instead of hardening, you soften. This helps *her* engage, connect, and soften. This simple shift enables us to reach our children's hearts with the lessons we need to teach.

A central belief in positive parenting is that showing a child that your boundaries are fixed, consistent, and unshakable proves your ability as a leader and builds respect. Showing that your love is also fixed, consistent, and unshakable builds a child's self-worth. A challenge when switching from traditional parenting to positive parenting is learning to remain soft while we maintain our boundaries because we've been so conditioned to harden.

HOW TO BUILD YOUR CHILD'S SELF-IMAGE:

- ❖ Show physical affection.
- ❖ Communicate that he is fun to be around.
- ❖ Use words of encouragement and affirmation.
- ❖ Let her know her opinions matter to you.
- ❖ Create a positive environment that allows him to be who he is.

❖ Instill a sense of belonging by creating tight family bonds with traditions and community involvement.
❖ Let her initiate play, and follow her lead.
❖ Help him find an activity he enjoys that allows him to blossom.
❖ Encourage appropriate expression of feelings.
❖ Give her responsibilities.

Think of a specific problem behavior that your child exhibits from time to time. How can you convey that the behavior is unacceptable but the child is not?

✏️
....

....

....

Do you show your child unconditional positive regard now? If so, how? Does your partner?

✏️
....

....

....

BUILD YOUR OWN SELF-IMAGE AND EMOTIONAL HEALTH AS WELL!

We know children imitate us, and if we are constantly berating ourselves and voicing our displeasure, this transfers to them. In an article titled "Twelve Ways to Raise a Confident Child," Dr. William Sears says, "In the early years, a child's concept of self is so intimately tied up with the mother's concept of herself that a sort of mutual self-worth building goes on. What image do you reflect to your child?" He also states that children translate your unhappiness with yourself to mean unhappiness with them, and as they get older, they can begin to feel responsible for your feelings.

To improve your own emotional health, make sure to:

1. Connect with friends.

    Whom can you call or visit today?

✐

....

2. Move your body.

    What exercise can you do today? Can you go for a walk or do a short yoga class?

✐

....

3. Find a hobby you enjoy.

    What did you used to love to do but haven't done in a while? Is there a new hobby you're interested in?

✐

....

4. Work on managing your own emotions. (You did this in chapter two!)

Write down a recent success.

....

5. Get enough sleep.

What is a practical way to do this? Set your phone to shut off at eleven p.m.? Take a nap when your child naps, even if the dishes go undone for another hour?

....

Build your self-image by:

1. Becoming aware of the beliefs you carry about yourself. Where did they come from?

....

2. Challenging those beliefs. Are they true?

....

3. Using positive self-talk. Today's affirmation is?

....

4. Listing something good that you've done for someone recently.

✎
....

5. Listing specific things your parents did to build your self-image.

✎
....

....

....

6. Listing specific things your parents did that weakened your self-image.

✎
....

....

....

7. Listing the strengths and achievements you feel your parents didn't acknowledge or build up when you were growing up. How could they have done better in your view?

✎
....

....

....

....

QUESTIONS FOR REFLECTION

1. What fears do you have about loving unconditionally? Are you afraid it will spoil your child? Reinforce bad behavior?

✏

....

....

....

2. As best you can evaluate, does your child have a negative or positive self-worth? Signs of positive self-worth are positive friendships, confidence, positive comments about oneself, and willingness to try new things. Signs of low self-esteem or a negative self-worth are avoiding challenges or quitting easily, socially withdrawing, making critical comments about oneself, and having difficulty accepting praise or criticism.

✏

....

....

3. Consider what you currently do to either build up or tear down your child, and ways you can improve in this area.

✏

....

....

....

4. Talk with your partner about ways that unconditional love and correction can coexist. Specifically, how can you correct your child in a way that says, "What you have done is wrong," rather than, "Who you are is wrong"?

🖎

....

....

....

JOURNAL SPACE

🖎

....

....

....

....

....

....

....

....

....

CHAPTER NINE

Trading Punishment for Solutions

Moving away from punishment seems to be the most difficult aspect of positive parenting for most people to grasp and implement, because they fear it means eliminating discipline. It is the *fear of permissiveness* that keeps many parents locked in punitive parenting. Think of it this way: Discipline is actually learning to manage oneself—learning to take responsibility for one's own emotions and behaviors, just like *we* had to do back in chapter two. If we want to have disciplined children, we have to teach them self-discipline. In positive parenting, we view discipline not as something we *do to* children but as something we *instill* in them. In chapter two, we were still working on our own self-discipline, learning to control our thoughts and reactions. If we are still learning in our twenties, thirties, forties, and beyond, perhaps we can have a little more understanding when the five-year-old child hasn't mastered this yet.

Here is the problem I have with punishment. It can actually rob kids of valuable lessons. It snatches away from them the opportunity to take responsibility for their behavior, fix their mistakes, learn from their choices, and grow from the experience. Children can't learn responsibility with a nose in the corner, and let's face it, they aren't actually sitting in that chair and making a plan for better behavior. What I propose isn't to free children from the responsibility of their actions (that's permissiveness) but to actually *hand the responsibility over to them* to do damage control, make amends, and learn better skills. Unfortunately, when we rely heavily on punishment for behavior management, children learn shame rather than responsibility—shame for being bad, for causing harm—without the chance to repair and learn. They get used to us "fixing" their mistakes for them with a five-minute time-out or the loss of a privilege for the day, and they don't learn how to develop and internalize discipline. They've "done the time," so it's now off their shoulders. Rather than imposing suffering on our kids when they make a mistake, let's resolve to help them work out the thoughts and emotions that are driving their behavior and repair any damage that was done, whether to property or to relationships.

Here's another problem I see with punishment, particularly separation-based discipline like time-out or sending kids to their room. I know we felt as a society that we were moving in the right direction by getting away from the physical punishment that has been proven to harm children. Time-out was popularized because of the work of B. F. Skinner, but even he admitted, "What's wrong with punishments is that they work immediately but give no long-term results." Sadly, we didn't understand that facing separation is actually a very wounding experience for young children and therefore isn't a step in the right direction at all. The reason it appears to work is actually very heart-wrenching. Children have a developmental need to be close to us, to seek attachment. When we force separation, it evokes feelings of alarm and panic. Developmental psychologist

Dr. Gordon Neufeld says, "When they are alarmed, they are moved to caution so it seems to us this is a good thing." It "works" because it brings up a great anxiety in children. They "behave" from a place of insecurity, feeling deep emotional unrest because they fear losing the attachment bond. This also evokes feelings of frustration, which leads to aggression problems, so while it may appear to work short-term, punishment can lead to deep emotional problems in children.

There are different forms of time-out, of course. It can be used as a positive tool in which a child is given the space and time to collect himself. The difference between punishment and a respectful tool is the intent and attitude of the parent. When the parent withdraws warmth, affection, and attention or uses it as a forced separation, it is punishment. When a parent lovingly provides the space and time for a child to regroup (think time-out in sports), it can be a positive tool. The difference is the message you're sending to the child. "I don't want to be around you until you're doing what I want" versus "I can see you need a bit of space to calm down and I'm here to help if you need me."

Let's look for a moment at the assumptions that lead us to punish our children. Could those negative messages we discussed before be playing a role in this in our minds? The idea that children will run wild if not ruled by the iron fist is a pretty prevalent belief in our culture. There's this perception that children will do bad things without the threat of a punishment hanging over them. We presume if we don't punish them, they won't be able to realize their potential, and this is the hook that catches parents' attention. We justify it as being in their best interest because of course we want them to be the best they can be.

But without punishment, how will you discipline? You will provide coaching and skills, and teach them to problem-solve. Something must take the place of punishment because of course children do need our guidance and correction. Failing to provide and enforce boundaries and correct bad behavior isn't positive or respectful. That's where permissiveness occurs. Removing punishment is not the same as removing boundaries. We'll look at how this plays out in this chapter. For now, what emotions are arising in you after reading this section?

✏️

....

....

....

What fears come up for you when you think of removing punishment from your parenting toolbox?

✏️

....

....

....

When you were a child, what types of punishment did you experience from your parents? What thoughts and feelings did these experiences bring out in you?

✏️

....

....

....

....

What could your parents have done differently at the time? How would that have made you feel—and what would you have taken away from those experiences instead?

✏️

....

....

....

By trading punishment for *solutions*, we teach children how to be thinkers and problem solvers. Instead of making them pay for wrongdoing, we encourage them and teach them how to right their wrongdoing and keep from repeating the same mistakes in the future. I want to be clear about consequences. Some say it's a matter of semantics—that *consequences* is really just another term for *punishment*. And it *can* be, but there is a distinct difference. It's all about intent and delivery. Any consequence given should be related to solving the problem and for the purpose of teaching responsibility, not simply to make the child suffer, and it should be delivered with kindness and empathy. When children are punished, their focus is not on their behavior but on how mean and unfair you are. With proper consequences, children learn something valuable rather than just suffering for their actions.

Following are a few examples of punishment versus consequences.

1. Let's say one of your child's daily responsibilities is to unpack and clean out her lunch box and thermos and repack it for the next day. If she doesn't do it, the consequence is having to eat school lunch the next day, whatever it may be. On a rushed Monday morning, she realizes she didn't pack her lunch. You could scold her, call her irresponsible, and even tell her she gets no TV time

tonight because she can't keep up with basic responsibilities, but then pack her lunch for her and send her on her way. Or you could say, "I'm sorry, sweetie. You'll have to eat school lunch today. I hope it's something good!" Eating school lunch is a consequence. Scolding and taking away TV privileges is punishment.

2. Your son is playing baseball with his friend in the backyard again despite your warnings that he could bust a window, which he does. You could ground him for a week, which would serve as punishment. Or you could have him work to earn the money to repair the window. This one is a little trickier because the intent and delivery of option two determines if your son sees it as a punishment or if he really learns a valuable lesson.

   a. "I cannot believe you disobeyed me again! And look what happened?! Mr. Willis has a broken window! That was so irresponsible of you! You're going to work hard every day until you've earned enough money to replace that window, and you're going to march over there and tell Mr. Willis how sorry you are!"

   b. "You must feel pretty bad about Mr. Willis's window. Accidents happen, but when we make a mistake, we have to own up to it and fix it. Thankfully, Mr. Willis said he'll let you work off the damages by mowing his lawn for a month. Owning up to it and repaying him are really responsible things to do. I'm proud of you."

   The difference between punishment and consequence sometimes is simply in what you choose to focus on or highlight—the bad choice or the bad kid.

3. Mary leaves her bike out instead of putting it in the garage. The bike gets damaged or stolen as a result. The consequence has already happened—she has no bike. Grounding her for leaving the bike out just adds insult to injury. It's an arbitrary punishment

that provides no real solution. Sometimes life is the best teacher, and we just need to allow the consequences to play out. If you run out and buy her a new bike, the lesson is lost. She can do chores to earn a new bike. This will probably make her care for it more once she gets it. You might have her post a reminder for herself at the door: DID YOU PUT YOUR BIKE AWAY? Working for a new bike and posting a note is a *solution*.

Think of an example of a punishment you've given your child. How effective was it? Were there any unintended messages or consequences? Can you think of a better solution now?

✏️
....
....
....

In *Positive Parenting*, I present the following five steps to solution-oriented discipline. Add your own notes to each step.

1. Look for the reason behind the behavior. Remember that the behavior is communicating something. What is it? Always ask yourself, "What is this behavior telling me?"

✏️
....
....
....

2. Discipline yourself first. Wait until you are calm and rational before you address your child and attempt to deal with the problem. Undisciplined parents can't effectively discipline a child. Think of some go-to phrases you can use, such as "I need a few minutes to myself, and then we'll talk about this" or "I'm going to give this some thought and we'll discuss it later."

✎

....

....

....

3. Connect with your child. This is a countercultural idea, connecting with a misbehaving kid. We generally believe this is the time to toughen up and withdraw to show our disapproval, but the basic human need for love and connection must be met before the brain is free to learn the lesson you want to teach. Connecting softens your child's heart toward you and allows your lesson to be internalized. How do you feel about this?

✎

....

....

....

4. Seek a solution. Teach your child to be a problem solver, to right her wrongs, and to repair relationships. This approach takes more time but serves her better than just making her serve time. Jot down a list of ideas for a solution to a recurring or typical problem.

✏️

....

....

....

5. Restore and reconnect. Make sure your child's self-worth is restored and he understands that mistakes are opportunities to learn and that a bad choice doesn't mean he's a bad person. Tell him how proud you are of him for working through the problem and that you admire the person he's becoming.

✏️

....

....

....

I list these six alternatives to punishment in *Positive Parenting*:

1. Take it away. Removing privileges for the sake of "making them suffer" is punishment, but there are times when taking something away is the logical solution. For example, you might take away a toy that your toddler keeps throwing so as to protect the walls or his sister's head. I once took away my son's iPad because he wasn't following the guidelines we had agreed upon

when we gave it to him. If something is being misused, it makes sense to take it away. I've also taken away items or games that my children were fighting over. I would say, "Your relationship is more important than this toy." The message was clear. Relationships are top priority, and if something is causing harm to the relationship, it goes. Once they came to a peaceful agreement, they got it back.

2. The peace table is a safe area where children can go to work through their conflicts. It's a place where they learn peaceful conflict resolution skills. This is commonly used in Montessori schools and can also be effective for inner conflict resolution. An upset child can come to the table, which has useful calming tools such as an hourglass to watch the sand, a glitter jar, or other peace objects. Teach the child to come to this space and watch the glitter or sand or close her eyes and breathe deeply. This isn't a place to angrily send a child but one to invite her into. It is also used to walk children through the steps of resolving a conflict by teaching them to take turns explaining why they are upset with each other. This teaches listening and communication skills. Give them the chance to come to an agreement and mediate, or offer solutions when necessary.

3. Pull over. Arguing in the car is a common complaint, and for good reason: It's distracting for the driver! When my children argue in the car, I simply pull to the side of the road if I can and sit quietly. For some kids, this works; others keep right on arguing. When my kids ask why I stopped, I simply state, "I can't concentrate on driving when you're fighting. I'll drive again when you're ready." Mine don't like sitting idly on the side of the road, so it's effective.

4. Have them write it out. I sometimes have my children sit with me and write out the family rule that has been violated. This helps commit it to memory. Once they write it out, I ask them to repeat it to me and we will discuss why this rule is in place. If a repair needs to be made in a relationship, I'll ask how they intend to make the repair.

5. Give grace. No matter how great a parent you are or how wonderfully behaved your children are, they will sometimes make mistakes or poor choices. It's part of being human, of growing and learning. Children don't always need a lecture or a consequence. Sometimes they're having a bad day and sometimes life is just plain hard. Learn when to give them a little grace.

6. Time-in is a great alternative to time-out. In time-in, you bring a child onto your lap or a calming area such as a peace table or a calm-down corner, where you have strategically placed several items to help your child calm down. Why? Because when children are angry or emotionally charged, they aren't able to access the rational part of their brain. They need to be able to do this before they can problem-solve. When calming has occurred, you can discuss the solution and practice new skills before you exit the space. "Show me three things you can do when you're angry and let's practice. One, stomp your feet. Go! Good. Now, two, jump up and down! High five! And three, take big dinosaur breaths. Good! Let's practice those three again. The next time you get angry with your friend, try these, okay?"

Are you still having a difficult time processing the idea that children don't need to be punished to learn from their mistakes and do better next time? Write out your fears and see if you can work them through to the end. What is the worst outcome of your fear, and is it likely or logical?

✐
....

....

....

....

....

QUESTIONS FOR REFLECTION

1. When your child misbehaves, who currently takes responsibility?

✐
....

....

2. Does solution-oriented discipline make sense to you? What might be the outcome for a child who receives punishment versus one who is given the responsibility to fix his own mistakes?

✐
....

....

3. Plan how you will intentionally respond—not react—to the behaviors that you find most challenging. Think of ways the problem can be solved. Ask your child to help solve the problem.

....
....
....
....

4. Are you willing to switch from time-out to time-in? What would that look like for a specific problem behavior you'd like your child to work on? Consider a two-month trial run to see how the situation changes.

....
....

JOURNAL SPACE

....
....
....
....
....

....

....

....

....

....

....

....

....

Top Parenting Challenges—And How to Use Proactive Parenting to Deal with Them

TELLING PEOPLE HOW to handle specific discipline problems is really not my thing. I believe that all children and families are unique, and expecting one piece of advice to work for everyone across the board is unrealistic. Rather, my goal is to empower and inspire parents to choose love, to listen to the whispers of their own hearts, to be proactive in learning about their child's brain and development, and to see the little person behind the behavior, always. With that said, I understand that it is helpful to have a frame of reference to move toward until you feel confident in your own approach and abilities. It is in the spirit of helping a friend that I offer this advice for dealing with specific common behavioral "problems." Please understand this is not a rule book! You know your child better than anyone else, and if you tap into your own knowing, it will guide you.

AGGRESSION

I recently surveyed a group of more than nine thousand parents, and I asked them what the top behaviors were that they struggled with the most. Landing at number one on that list is aggression. When we observe a child behaving aggressively, we often view this behavior as naughty, inconsiderate, or mean. This moves us to want to punish the child's action without giving thought to the feelings driving it. It helps to understand that, developmentally, young children cannot feel big emotions and simultaneously think about their actions. This requires left-brain logic to pair with right-brain emotion, and that integration takes time to mature and cannot be punished into a child.

Looking behind the aggression, you'd find a feeling of frustration driving it, and it is addressing the frustration (not punishing the aggression) that helps a child move to good behavior. Many times, we choose a method of discipline that only increases a child's frustration level, thereby increasing the occurrence of aggression. We think the child is simply pushing back or being obstinate or very unruly, which requires even more punishment, when in actuality our punishment is fueling the fires we are trying to extinguish.

There are many ways we can help an immature child to manage his behavior during times of frustration until his brain allows for more self-control. **To be proactive on aggression:**

1. Be aware of what you are modeling. If you're aggressive when agitated or angry, your child will see this as an appropriate behavior.
2. Ensure that the discipline you are using isn't causing anxiety or adding to your child's frustration. Punishment only adds to the negative feelings that drive poor behavior.

3. Give plenty of positive attention. Dr. Neufeld tells us that children "need more from us than they seek." If we keep their emotional tanks full, they'll be less frustrated.

4. Help your child cry when she is frustrated or upset. When children cry, these negative feelings are discharged through the tears.

5. Involve him in caring for a new baby. To reduce feelings of jealousy and anxieties about losing Mommy's time, involve your child in the care of your new baby as much as possible, and make sure to still make time for one-on-one quality time with him when the baby naps.

6. Help your child build a positive self-image by talking about the good qualities you see in her. Build her up! Don't use language such as *mean, naughty,* or *aggressive* to or in front of her. Remember it's the lack of maturity that's a problem, not the child.

7. Give him language for his emotions. Help him to identify his feelings and support him to express himself in a way that doesn't hurt or harm him, another, or property.

8. Ask your child where she feels frustration and anger in her body. Ask her to draw you a picture to illustrate this. Discuss what these emotions feel like when they are just beginning and when they peak and how to recognize them when they are beginning to build.

When do you typically notice your child becoming aggressive? What occurrences lead to the frustration?

✏️

....

....

Watch your child closely over the next few days. Look for signs of frustration. What clues does she give that frustration is building?

✎

....

....

Recognizing the signs will help you to be proactive in handling your child's aggressive behavior. You can help your child move from frustration to tears of sadness and back to positive emotions by remaining connected, providing empathy, and holding your boundary.

Does your typical response to aggressive behavior add to or reduce frustration for your child?

✎

....

WHEN AGGRESSION HAPPENS

The five steps to solution-oriented discipline discussed in the previous chapter are a good go-to for all behavioral problems. You may want to write down these steps and keep them handy. Let's go through what that looks like when your child is aggressive.

Step 1 is looking for the reason behind the behavior. Ask yourself, "What is my child frustrated about right now?" This information will guide your next action. For example, if he's frustrated because he's overtired, it may be best to leave the activity and go home or provide some quiet time. If he's frustrated because he's not getting his way, the next action is to hold the boundary with empathy.

Step 2 is disciplining yourself. According to the parents I surveyed, seeing their children being aggressive was mostly likely to bring out their own aggression. They became verbally or physically aggressive with their kids in order to discipline their aggressive behavior. Bringing your own frustration and aggression into the mix isn't helpful, so discipline yourself first. Remove your child from any harmful situation and take a few moments to collect yourself before you proceed.

Step 3 is connecting with your child. Again, this isn't a reward for bad behavior but the avenue through which you can reach his heart. When we understand that empathy, kindness, warmth, and connection are not carrots that can be dangled in front of children, handed out only when they behave to our liking, and provide for the very real emotional needs of a growing, learning, loving human being, we can stop being afraid to show love at all times. You connect by showing regard for their experience, being empathetic to their feelings, and remaining gentle. You can do this while holding whatever boundary you need to hold, and it gets easier with practice.

Step 4 is to seek a solution. Can this particular frustration be avoided? Can you be proactive the next time and provide food or a nap before an outing? What does your child need to learn from this experience? What will help him learn that?

Step 5 is restoring the relationship and your child's sense of worth along with reconnecting with your little one. Tell her, "You were frustrated today and pushed down your brother. Everyone makes mistakes sometimes. I'm still really proud of the wonderful person you are. You make my heart happy. Do you want to play a game together?"

NOTES ON AGGRESSION:

....

....

....

....

....

....

....

....

....

WHINING

Whining was the second most difficult behavior according to the parents I polled. While some parents view this as persistent begging for something, others see it as a particular voice a child uses. Both types of whining can certainly grate on a parent's nerves.

The whining in "a different voice" is basically upgraded crying. It still provokes that same visceral reaction in us that crying provokes— we want to make it *stop*! The difference is, when we heard our babies cry, we saw a helpless baby, so we reacted lovingly. When we hear our big kids "cry" in this whiny voice, we typically see a child trying to manipulate us, and this becomes our perception, because remember, how we perceive our kids determines how we treat them. When we switch from feeling manipulated to seeing a child trying to get his need met, we can avoid being triggered by it.

What emotional response does whining evoke in you? Why do you think this happens?

✏

....

....

When your child whines, what has been your response in the past?

✏

....

Be proactive about whining by:

❖ Offering choices. When we give children some power over their day-to-day lives, they feel less powerless. And that often means less whining.
❖ Validating emotions. "I understand you're disappointed. Need a hug?"
❖ Teaching the difference between a strong voice and a whiny voice.
❖ Invoking your child's imagination. If she's whining over going to the park, but it's a rainy day, say something like, "I bet you wish we could make the rain stop with a silly dance and use a giant hair dryer to dry up the world! Would a hair dryer work?"

Plenty of parenting experts will tell you to ignore a whining child. I'm not an expert, but my reasoning is that ignoring the people we love never does anything positive for the relationship. Sure, you might choose to ignore the whiny voice once you've said no firmly and moved on, but that's quite different from ignoring the child. In fact, you're moving on with your own cheerful attitude and tone, being just as kind and loving as you always are, *not* pretending the child doesn't exist.

WHEN WHINING HAPPENS:

1. Listen. Often children just want to feel heard. We all need to feel that our opinions matter.
2. Look for the reason behind the behavior. Have you tattooed this on your body somewhere by now? Meet the need behind the behavior and the behavior is likely to dissipate.
3. Provide lots of preemptive cuddles and laughter. I tell you, it's the cure for many ills.
4. Teach negotiation skills. What?! Yes, it's a valuable skill to learn in life, and we too often shut it down to prove our parental authority. Teach her to state her needs in a respectful manner and how to work to find a solution that works for everyone involved. When she knows you'll take her seriously, she'll lose the need to whine. This doesn't mean you give her what she wants all the time, just that you hear her out and give her a real chance to explain. As long as she's being respectful and kind about it, she's building life skills—and you're building a bond of trust together.
5. If you really do mean no, then don't give in. When you've truly listened to his side, taken it into consideration, and determined

that the answer is still no, simply say, "You've already asked, and I've already answered." When this is the consistent response, the whining will eventually stop.

NOTES ON WHINING:

....

....

....

....

....

....

....

....

....

NOT LISTENING

Not listening came in at number three in the list of most annoying behaviors that cause parents to lose their cool. And by not listening, I think they meant "not doing what I say the minute I say it." We want children to cooperate without us having to ask ten times, and that's reasonable. Ironically, we usually resort to tactics that are more about control than cooperation. Punishment or the threat of punishment may compel a child to act in that moment, but it increases feelings of frustration, which, as we have learned, can lead to aggression.

Of course, this is probably an opportune moment to think about our expectations of children. As I'm sitting here writing this book, my husband came in and said he needed my help with something. I told him I'd be just a minute. That minute turned into forty-five because I became engrossed in my work. We often ask our kids to do something when they are engrossed in their work, whatever it may be. In our adult world, we have deadlines to meet and households to run, so completing a video game level or a round of play may not seem important to us, but remember that play *is* the work of childhood. That idea was attributed to three different people in my web search, so I don't know who really said it, but it's true nonetheless. What we sometimes perceive as willful disobedience or "not listening" is really just a child having his full attention elsewhere.

We also expect children to feel the urgency that we feel and have the priorities we have, but they don't. I might want my son to hurry up and get his room cleaned up before company comes over, but he's not likely to hurry up and do anything (because do children ever?), and he doesn't see the value in a spotless room for the company. That's not to say he shouldn't clean his room, but to point out an obvious fact that we sometimes forget—they are their own people. It also points out the different ways we request a child to clean his room and, for example, a husband to straighten up the garage. Parents tend to ask adults politely and bark orders at children and *maybe it's in the barking where we lose the cooperation*. I can promise you that if my husband came in here and demanded I stop writing and fold my laundry "right this instant," I'd let the basket sit there for three days because *rudeness invites defiance*. I know sometimes we start out asking politely and then resort to barking because it doesn't get done quickly enough, and sometimes we go straight to barking because we anticipate the not listening to occur, but this is something to be mindful of.

When asking your child to do a chore or take a bath (or whatever she "doesn't listen" to), do you ask with the same tone of respect you use with adults?

✐

....

Where do you have the most trouble with your child not listening? How might you change your approach to get out of the pattern?

✐

....

Fortunately, there are ways to increase cooperation. Here's how to be proactive about not listening:

❖ Focus on keeping the connection strong. When your relationship is in good standing, your child will be much more cooperative.

❖ Be mindful of transitions and give the child appropriate time to comply. We live in our hurried adult state, but our kids don't!

❖ Use a firm but respectful tone at a conversational distance. It's best to get your child's eye contact before you make a request.

❖ Use "I want" statements rather than "will you" statements. "Will you pick up your toys" leaves an option for no. It's a question, and that's what kids hear. "I want you to pick up your toys" makes it clear.

❖ Guide her in the direction she needs to go. If you asked her to pick up her toys and she didn't, take her by the hand, lead her to the toy mess, and point to the basket where they go. If you keep repeating yourself, you're going to get frustrated and it'll be harder to remain positive.

Children are naturally inclined to follow those who have their hearts. When a child is frequently defiant, ignores your requests, treats you disrespectfully, and so on, it's a sign that the relationship is in trouble. This doesn't mean that a child who is deeply connected to you will jump the minute you say jump, but he will be much more cooperative and pleasant with you. If there is a relational problem, it doesn't mean you've done something terribly wrong. Even just being too busy for quality time for a couple of days can leave a child feeling a bit off. If you see signs of relationship trouble, ask yourself:

❖ How much quality time have I been giving him?
❖ Have I been present and engaged?
❖ Have I been treating her with respect or barking orders?
❖ Have we had hurt feelings toward each other that haven't been repaired?
❖ Am I being reasonable with my expectations?

NOTES ON NOT LISTENING:

🖎 ....

....

....

....

....

....

....

....

TANTRUMS

Tantrums, oh tantrums. Coming in at number four on the "drives parents bonkers" list, it is really our perception of tantrums, not the tantrums themselves, that pushes our buttons. We often perceive them as defiance, manipulation, or bratty behavior. During a true tantrum, kids have no control over it. Once they've hit the emotional boiling point, they explode and there's nothing you can do but wait out the storm and offer some consolation. During these emotional meltdowns, reasoning with or punishing a child isn't helpful. Tantrums aren't bad behavior but an emotional response, and your child just needs your loving support to help him pull himself together. You can hold your boundary and not buy the toy that caused the emotional meltdown while still providing comfort.

Sure, some big kids have "tantrums" that are strategic in nature. In this case, the child is in control (not in emotional overwhelm) and is acting upset to get her way. Yes, in this case the child is trying to manipulate you, but you don't have to get sucked into a fight. She's resorted to this because she doesn't know how best to communicate with you what she wants. You'll get through it much quicker and feel better about yourself if you remain loving, and the most loving thing to do is to hold your boundaries and remain calm and kind. Don't give in as a result of this type of tantrum unless you want a repeat of it. When she realizes this isn't going to get her what she wants, it'll stop. However, she needs coaching on how better to express what she wants without resorting to such a strategy.

Can you think of a time your child had a true tantrum? What about a strategic tantrum? It's fairly easy for parents to tell the difference, and each one requires a different approach. True tantrums need lots of love and comfort, while strategic tantrums need boundaries and coaching.

The common advice is to treat every tantrum the same way: Ignore the child while it occurs so as to show you cannot be manipulated by such nonsense. Ignoring a child who is in true emotional distress is a very unkind thing to do. Ignoring a child who is having a rant is going to add more frustration to the concoction of emotions, which might push it to a true tantrum. He wants to be heard, which is the reason for the fit in the first place. Hear him, empathize, and hold boundaries.

How to be proactive about tantrums:

- As best you can, make sure your child has had enough rest, food, and physical activity.
- Be aware of tantrum triggers and prevent or avoid them.
- Teach emotional awareness by giving her words to describe her feelings.
- Establish an atmosphere in which your child feels heard, accepted, and understood, and in which the lines of communication are open. A child who feels that his parent often shuts him down without hearing him out is more likely to resort to a strategic tantrum.

NOTES ON TANTRUMS:

....

....

....

....

....

....

....

....

....

BACK TALK

Back talk is number five according to my poll. All children, even the most connected and secure ones, will occasionally challenge their parents. Again, having a loving and respectful relationship will reduce the chances of this becoming a big problem, but all children are different, and I think personality certainly plays a part. It's important to note that in early childhood, children are just learning that they are separate beings from their parents. The need for autonomy and to express one's own thoughts and feelings often is mistaken for back talk. So when "Make your bed" is answered with "no," our feathers get ruffled, but this is a normal part of development. It's our reactions that turn some molehills into mountains.

We want our children to have a voice. We want them to be able to assert themselves when necessary. We all hope they'll say, "I don't want to do this right now," to the boyfriend or no to the friend offering drugs. While it's certainly easier for parents to shut it down immediately, I think it's more beneficial to children to teach them how to communicate respectfully and be assertive appropriately. Learning to effectively communicate her side of things is a good skill to have, so let her practice it sometimes.

To be proactive about back talk:

❖ Model respectful communication. Teach her to state her views respectfully.
❖ When requests are nonnegotiable, state them as requests, not questions.
❖ Play games such as beat the timer. Make dull tasks fun.
❖ Be the "captain of the ship," as parenting educator Susan Stiffelman calls it. Consider how a captain handles the ship when a

storm comes and the seas get rough. He or she doesn't run about yelling but stays at the wheel, steady, focused, and calm. If the captain starts freaking out, the passengers will, too! Be the confident leader who doesn't get ruffled by the storms.

❖ Hold your boundaries. Don't allow your child to treat you disrespectfully or talk to you rudely. Say, "I won't allow you to speak to me that way. I'll be happy to discuss this when you are able to do so respectfully. You can go to your room and calm down."

❖ Teach your child the positive communication skills we discussed in chapter four.

❖ Apologize if you've been disrespectful or too controlling to your child in the past, and set a new standard of respect.

❖ Be careful not to be too controlling (never giving the child any control) or too permissive (letting the child have too much control). When parents are too controlling, children will feel the need to push back and angle for some control. If parents are too permissive, children won't honor boundaries and will believe everything is negotiable.

WHEN BACK TALK HAPPENS:

Here are my three keys for handling back talk.

1. Listen to the feelings behind the words and discern what is really motivating the child.

2. Empathize, which shows that you listen and care about what he feels and wants *while still holding the limit*. This means if you said, "No, you can't go out with your friends tonight," for a good reason, then you don't flip and allow him to go to avoid the argument. You

simply say, "I understand you're feeling upset because you can't go tonight."

3. Listen and keep an open mind. If you're willing to hear her out and possibly even change your mind after a good debate about it, you're not a weak parent. You're flexible and reasonable. If it's really nonnegotiable, state so respectfully, and politely end the conversation.

NOTES ON BACK TALK:

What are the top behaviors that push your buttons? How can you handle them better with the knowledge you have now?

✎
....
....
....
....
....

JOURNAL SPACE

✎
....
....
....
....
....
....
....
....
....

FINAL NOTES

The most important things you've learned from this book are:

✏️
....

....

....

....

....

Have you been inspired by this book? In what way?

✏️
....

....

....

....

....

What specific passages struck you as significant, profound, or memorable? Collect your favorites here:

NOTES

1. Eanes, Rebecca. "When Your Toddler Defies You, Love is the Answer." *Motherly*. N.p., n.d. https://www.mother.ly/child/when-your-toddler-defies -you-love-is-the-answer.

2. Sroufe, L. A. "From Infant Attachment to Promotion of Adolescent Autonomy: Prospective, Longitudinal Data on the Role of Parents in Development." *Parenting and the Child's World: Influences on Academic, Intellectual, and Social-emotional Development*, edited by J. G. Borkowski, S. L. Ramey, and M. Bristol-Power. New York: Psychology Press, 2001.

3. Cook, Eliza, and Rachel Dunifon. *Do Family Meals Really Make a Difference?* Ithaca, NY: Cornell Cooperative Extension, 2012.

4. Winch, Ph.D., Guy. "Does Self-esteem Function as an Emotional Immune System?" *Psychology Today*, 26 June 2013. https://www.psychologytoday.com /blog/the-squeaky-wheel/201306/does-self-esteem-function-emotional-immune -system.

RECOMMENDATIONS
FOR FURTHER READING

This section contains articles and books that have either been mentioned in this book or that I feel will deepen your understanding of positive parenting and the science behind it.

Books

Eanes, Rebecca. *Positive Parenting: An Essential Guide.* New York: TarcherPerigee, 2016.

Kohn, Alfie. *Unconditional Parenting: Moving from Rewards and Punishments to Love and Reason.* New York: Atria, 2006.

Markham, Dr. Laura. *Peaceful Parent, Happy Kids: How to Stop Yelling and Start Connecting.* New York: TarcherPerigee, 2015.

Neufeld, PhD, Gordon, and Gabor Maté, MD. *Hold On to Your Kids: Why Parents Need to Matter More Than Peers.* New York: Ballantine, 2014.

Pantley, Elizabeth. *The No-Cry Sleep Solution for Toddlers and Preschoolers: Gentle Ways to Stop Bedtime Battles and Improve Your Child's Sleep.* New York: McGraw-Hill, 2005.

Siegel, MD, Daniel J., and Tina Payne Bryson, PhD. *No-Drama Discipline: The Whole-Brain Way to Calm the Chaos and Nurture Your Child's Developing Mind.* New York: Bantam, 2016.

Siegel, MD, Daniel J., and Tina Payne Bryson, PhD. *The Whole-Brain Child.* London: Robinson, 2012.

Articles

McLeod, Saul. "Carl Rogers." *Simply Psychology.* N.p., 2014. https://www.simply psychology.org/carl-rogers.html.

McLeod, Saul. "Mary Ainsworth." *Simply Psychology.* N.p., 2014. https://www .simplypsychology.org/mary-ainsworth.html.

McLeod, Saul. "Maslow's Hierarchy of Needs." *Simply Psychology.* N.p., 16 Sept. 2016. https://simplypsychology.org/maslow.html.

Payne Bryson, Tina, PhD. "Upstairs and Downstairs Tantrums." N.p., 05 Aug. 2011. http://www.tinabryson.com/tina-payne-bryson-phd-1/667.

ABOUT THE AUTHOR

Rebecca Eanes is the founder of Positive-Parents.org and creator of the popular Facebook community Positive Parenting: Toddlers and Beyond. She is the author of *The Newbie's Guide to Positive Parenting* and *Positive Parenting: An Essential Guide,* as well as coauthor of *Positive Parenting in Action.* She is a contributing editor to *Creative Child* magazine and parenting editor at *Motherly.*

As a mother who made the paradigm shift from traditional parenting to positive parenting, Rebecca shares inspiration and her hard-earned wisdom daily through her rapidly growing Facebook community. Seeing how the power of emotional connection transformed her own family inspired Rebecca to share this message with other parents in hopes that they, too, may find more joy and peace.

She is married to her high school sweetheart and loves capturing miracle moments every day with her two sons. She is nestled in the beautiful Appalachian Mountains with her family and an assortment of furry companions.

FOREWORD BY DR. LAURA MARKHAM,
author of *PEACEFUL PARENT, HAPPY KIDS*

POSITIVE
PARENTING

— AN ESSENTIAL GUIDE —

Ending the Power Struggles
and Reconnecting from the Heart

REBECCA EANES, Creator of Positive-Parents.org